GETTING THERE FROM HERE

Helps on Divine Guidance

GETTING THERE FROM HERE

Helps on Divine Guidance

Cecil Murphey

WORD BOOKS
PUBLISHER
WACO, TEXAS

GETTING THERE FROM HERE
Copyright © 1981 by Word Incorporated, Waco, Texas 76796. All
rights reserved. No portion of this book may be reproduced in any
form, except for brief quotations in reviews, without the written
permission of the publisher.

ISBN 0-8499-0196-0
Library of Congress Catalog Card No: 80-54547
Printed in the United States of America

To Victor, who knows the reasons

Contents

Introduction

Our writers' group listened intently as Edna beamed, "I've sold it! My book! And it's my first sale! I wrote the book, then refused to mail it out until I knew I'd found the right publisher. I prayed for two weeks. Then yesterday—three months after I mailed it— I received a contract and a check!"

Edna rhapsodized on how the Lord had led her into the whole project. While she never said it in so many words, she conveyed the impression that if other Christian writers prayed more carefully before submitting manuscripts they would avoid rejection slips.

Edna frequently exhorted novice scribes with such verses as Matthew 7:7: "Ask, and it will be given you; seek, and you will find; knock, and it will be opened to you." That settled it for her. She had asked, received guidance from the Holy Spirit, followed that enlightenment—and it had paid off. Therefore, she had been using the proper method.

Two years later, after concerted prayer, Edna submitted a second manuscript. She received an almost immediate rejection. I restrained myself, but I really felt like asking, "What went wrong with your guidance?"

I also wanted to tell her, "Edna, I always pray before sending out manuscripts, yet I've received my share of nonacceptances." But, again, I kept silent.

My writer friend went through a severe depression when five additional publishers also rejected her manuscript. (She sold it to the seventh.) If she had been on the Lord's listening line, Edna reasoned, she could have avoided wasting two years between the first and seventh publishers. She would not have spent more than thirty dollars in postage and envelopes, and she could have saved herself a lot of anxiety and heartache. Guilt engulfed Edna, and she almost quit writing.

I've since wondered whether Edna and others like her have misunderstood the whole concept of divine guidance. Their attitudes depict a God quite different from the one I perceive from reading Scripture. For them, he becomes almost a great genie whom we keep tucked within the pages of the Bible and who comes out to offer directions for our immediate fulfillment in life. His responsibility centers on keeping committed Christians happy, blessed, and prosperous.

No one talks that kind of theology, of course. But, as a member of the Christian family for a quarter of a century, I've seen much of this attitude in action. *I've recognized it in myself!*

For the first few years after my conversion I would pray and expect an immediate answer. After obeying the guidance I received, I would expect a euphoric experience. Sometimes it didn't happen. Then, when guidance didn't come, or when acting upon that guidance didn't produce an emotional high, I had a ready-made answer—the devil was working against me.

It took me many years to come to grips with the whole subject of guidance. I've learned (often the hard way). I've rethought my attitudes. I've changed. That's largely why I'm writing this book—so that I can share my insights on knowing and following the will of God.

1.

Getting It Together With God

For the past two years I've been asking a lot of questions about guidance. I started questioning as I read the success stories of people who prayed. These people received miraculous answers (and I don't oppose miracles!). But always?

I've often wanted to ask about their not-so-startling answers. What about the times they prayed and life blew up in their faces?

Other questions troubled me. Does God continually desire our instant achievement? Does he will for us to go from one delirious mountaintop experience to the next? Is it only the devil who drags us into the low spots in life?

While no specific Bible verses answer those kinds of questions, reading the biblical accounts of the lives of the great saints at least indicates how God works in the lives of his people.

What about King David—called the apple of God's eye—who prayed often for guidance? ("Evening and morning and at noon I utter my complaint and moan, and he will hear my voice," Ps. 55:17, among others.) Yet that same praying man spent much of his adult life fleeing the wrath of King Saul.

Paul's impressive revelations, which excelled those of ordinary believers, led him onward—but onward to suffering, shipwreck, imprisonment, and attempts on his life.

What about Moses? Joseph? Jeremiah? Hosea?

In our Western world, on the other hand, God has particularly blessed us with high standards of living, relative

11

comfort, easy mobility, and religious freedom. As a result, many of us seem to have the subconscious idea that if God leads us we'll not have problems or setbacks.

Then, when setbacks do hit us, confusion takes over and we wail, "Why me, God? Why me?"

We have developed what I call the "Prosperity Doctrine." We anticipate enrichment and well-being to result when we follow Jesus Christ. We're also quite prepared to back up our expectations with Scripture.

This kind of thinking originated (so far as I can determine) in the early 1950s, when a famous evangelist, now dead, was eating in a restaurant. He had ordered the cheapest meal—two hamburgers—because he believed God wanted him to live frugally. As he munched on his tasteless hamburger, he saw two very worldly looking men at a nearby table. Overhearing snatches of their conversation, he concluded they had no relationship with God.

The evangelist then noticed what they were eating—magnificent, sizzling steaks. He later told people, "I decided that from that day on I'd never eat hamburger again. It's not right for God's people to live as paupers while the children of the devil enjoy all the good things our Father created."

He quoted 3 John 2—a scripture to which he referred often after that. In the King James version it reads, "Beloved, I wish above all things that thou mayest prosper and be in health, even as thy soul prospereth."

"See," he would say, pointing to the verse, "God wants us to prosper. It's his will for us to have the best. He wants the best for us in every area of life."

He shaped his theology on that verse, as did others who followed after him. Unfortunately, the verse doesn't sound so promising when read from other translations.*

Perhaps we don't all endorse such a naïve view of life, but many of our prayers and testimonies indicate that we expect to move from abundantly joyful feelings to additional highs. We

---

* My dear friend, I pray that everything may go well with you, and that you may be in good health—as I know you are well in spirit (TEV).

assume it is our right to receive emotional and material blessings.

My own experience, however, contradicts that viewpoint. I don't enjoy hardship. I never ask for problems or burdens. But I grow more convinced over the years that many lessons in our spiritual growth are learned only through hardship and suffering.

Reading the Bible and living as a Christian convinces me that God's will doesn't work like magazine advertisements—the kind that proclaim we'll lose up to fifteen pounds in two weeks, or grow hair on a bald head in four weeks, or become qualified computer experts in ten months. God doesn't hold out those automatic guarantees.

He does promise that when we seek him, he will be found.

And if we're going to get it all together with God, if we're going to understand guidance, we have to begin with God—not ourselves.

Starting with God doesn't mean all the answers will be clear to us. He's a supernatural God. He's also elusive at times. Just when we've nearly figured out all his operating principles, we realize that there's more to God we don't yet understand. But there are some things we know about God that can help us understand how he leads us. When we pray for guidance, the answers may become more satisfying if we bear in mind four facts:

1. *God wills for us to mature.* We often mature after first stumbling. For instance, Jesus warned Peter of his three-time denial. He could have said, "Peter, I want you to be careful. I'm going to be betrayed by Judas and, when you see me standing before Pilate, you'll be asked by onlookers if you're one of my followers. You'll be tempted to deny you even know me. I'm telling you now so that you can fortify yourself."

Jesus did warn Peter. But the disciple never really heard the Master's warning. And he failed in the crucial hour.

But Peter also matured through that ordeal. He learned he was fallible. He realized that, as much as he loved Jesus, he could still yield to the impulse of saving himself first.

2. *God wants us to overcome.* Interestingly, although this concept appears all through the Bible (e.g., 1 Cor. 15:57; Rev.

2:7), we still seek God for directions to keep us out of harm, danger, or testing. Then we tend to become angry with God if anything breaks up our pleasant lifestyles.

Overcoming can happen only when we fight and win! Overcoming applies to those swept into battle, but it holds no meaning for people who sit at the sidelines and continually pray for God to take them away from problems and remove all their difficulties.

In the early 1970s I became pastor of a church in a changing community. Formerly the home of comfortable, middle-class whites, it was rapidly becoming a black community with only a smattering of whites left. During that transitional period, our congregation began moving out, some losing money on their property. Since many had no one to whom they could lash out in anger, I, their pastor, often received the brunt of it. Others accused me of manipulating to make it an integrated church, whether they liked it or not. Some of the most religious people in the congregation said some unreligious things.

I'm years past that experience—and it was one of the most painful times in my life. Yet today, looking back, I believe myself to be a stronger person and a more effective Christian leader because of having struggled through the situation in that church.

Five times during the last year I was there,* pulpit committees approached me about filling their vacant pastorates. Two offers tempted me, but I felt I had to stay with the people.

The last months proved to be the most painful. It was like sitting at the bedside of a dying patient, mourning and yet unable to do anything except hold the patient's hand. Yet, by God's grace, I came out of the ordeal stronger and more committed to Christ. It was a battle I had to fight in order to be an overcomer.

3. *God wants us to strengthen others.* In order to do that we need to experience personal growth. We have to endure suffering first.

I learned that fact firsthand. For years, I had preached funeral

---

*We finally accepted our inability as a white congregation to minister to a black community, and turned the property over to a black church.

sermons, talked to the lonely, and offered comfort. It was my duty as a minister, and I had done the best I knew how. Then, within a period of eighteen months, four members of my immediate family (including both parents) died. And I grieved.

As a result of my own heartache, I became more understanding and sensitive toward others going through periods of grief. I believe that's part of what the apostle Paul means in 2 Corinthians 1:3–4, when he refers to the "God of all comfort, who comforts us in all our affliction, so that we may be able to comfort those who are in any affliction, with the comfort with which we ourselves are comforted by God."

4. *God wants us to be like Jesus Christ.* Romans 8:29 says, "For those whom he foreknew he also predestined to be conformed to the image of his Son." Hebrews 5:8–9 reads, "Although he was a Son, he learned obedience through what he suffered; and being made perfect he became the source of eternal salvation to all who obey him."

God sent Jesus to save. But he saved after being persecuted. He experienced betrayal by a disciple, rejection by others, misunderstanding by all—and then he made the supreme sacrifice at Calvary.

Jesus never escaped the hardships. He knew he had to wear a martyr's crown before receiving the king's diadem.

Thinking of Jesus makes me wonder if God really guides us to escape hardship . . . always.

Perhaps getting it together with God means obedience. It holds no guarantee of ease, prosperity, or blessing. It does promise peace, eternal life, and God's presence. That's what Jesus had. That's all the apostle Paul asked for.

But sometimes we ask for more.

I remember an incident during my military days, shortly after I became a Christian. Wayne slept a few bunks away from me. We often talked about the Lord, and one evening he made a profession of faith.

I had great hopes for his spiritual growth, but Wayne never really progressed, although he attended church services with me and even read his Bible. One day I talked to him.

He sat on his bunk and tears filled his eyes. "For weeks, I've been fighting God," he said. "I've had so much kidding from the men I work with, and all kinds of doubts." He went on to explain that he kept expecting God to give him quick answers to coworkers' taunts, and he remained tongue-tied. He had hoped for a greater degree of happiness, and his fiancée had written him a "Dear John" letter.

He finally looked straight at me. "I guess I kept looking for the wrong things. But this morning I made a decision. I've decided that I'm going to follow the Lord . . . whatever it takes."

What about us? Instead of yearning only for the apparent good things, maybe we ought to consider the price tag. Sometimes following Jesus is a costly choice.

But, like Wayne, we can say, "I'm going to follow the Lord . . . whatever it takes."

2.

What's God's Will For Me, Anyway?

"I wish I knew what to do, Lena said. "If only God would show me his will, then I'd have a sense of direction."

As I listened to Lena's confusion, I realized that I'd heard those words before. Most of us, when we get serious about our Christian commitment, talk in those terms. We don't always use the same words, but we speak of knowing God's will, of discovering it, of being sure of his guidance. There's something right about that attitude. It puts us in line with biblical people such as the apostle Paul. The famed apostle struggled to know how God was leading his missionary activities. On one occasion (see Acts 16:6–10), he tried to go into several different geographic areas. Each time God held up a stop sign. For a period of time, the apostle apparently didn't know what God wanted; he seemed to understand only what God *didn't* want.

Then he received a dream (a "night vision" in some translations). In this dream, a man from the area which is now the modern country of Greece appeared and pleaded, "Come to Macedonia—to my country." The apostle went.

Somehow we think of his going to Greece as the final chapter of a story. It's almost like a filmmaker's scenario. We have the cameras do a fade-in scene of the clouds with the sun bursting through, and a magnificent chorus makes the universe reverberate with strains of the "Hallelujah Chorus."

If we read a little more in the sixteenth chapter of Acts, however, we discover something quite different! As Handel's beautiful music declares, Jesus is "King of Kings, and Lord of Lords," and we affirm as truly as ever that "He will reign forever and ever." But while Jesus reigns—look what happens to the apostle! He's thrown into prison. He's beaten. A miraculous earthquake occurs, and he's eventually set free, but that's not the major point of the episode. The point is, the poor man suffered for the sake of Jesus Christ! He didn't simply march into glorious bliss forever.

Paul prayed. He sought guidance. And everything *didn't* work out smoothly. Yet, even in the midst of his suffering, the apostle Paul never seemed to doubt the Holy Spirit's leadership. He even sang and prayed in prison.

Perhaps the apostle Paul understood implications of God's will that many of us haven't. And so we ask, "What does it mean to know God's will?"

That is the basic question, the one we have to start with. And perhaps instead of thinking always of God's will *for me*, we might first look at it from God's own perspective—as much as we human beings can.

When we talk about God's will, most of us easily enough acknowledge that God has a plan. It's an overarching, through-the-ages plan that won't be defeated or frustrated. He'll accomplish his purposes.

But God's plan is also very specific—it includes every one of his children. By that I don't mean merely that God decrees we are to live godly lives. I mean that he plans for each of us to become finished products—not merely what we are now, but holy and perfect. At present we're only in the construction stage.

This became clear to me in a situation that occurred at Riverdale Presbyterian Church, where I am pastor. Our congregation voted to erect a multipurpose building. I studied the blueprints carefully and had a general idea of how the building would look. Then we began the construction. Every few days I'd walk through the building-in-progress and notice the changes. When the roof was finished, and the contractors had laid the floor, the building looked quite different from what I had been able to grasp from the line drawings. Then we moved into the finished building, and its beauty exceeded my expectations.

Until I saw the completed product, I was never quite able to visualize the finished effect, no matter how hard I tried.

That's how I see God's will. We're all human, limited by our finiteness. There's no way any of us can see everything ahead. We never know what God is going to work out in our lives. We never know what paths will cross ours.

For example, my denomination once appointed me to a committee on world hunger. I attended several meetings, felt nothing was happening but talk, and decided not to go back to the next session. But the morning of that meeting, as I prayed about my decision, it seemed right to attend.

Not being eager to go, I arrived a few minutes late. The only vacant place in the room was next to a man I'd never seen before. During the meeting, he introduced himself and said that his name was Bruce.

That was the beginning of one of the richest friendships I've ever experienced. From that time on, Bruce and I saw each other often; our families planned outings together. Most important of all, he was a friend who always had time to listen.

I share this because it points out to me how God operates. Because we can't always grasp his plans in advance, we often understand only after they have unfolded.

When I talk about God's will *for me*, I can rely on four things:

1. *God's will is never capricious.* That means God has a plan. The apostle Paul wrote, "He chose us in him before the foundation of the world, that we should be holy and blameless before him" (Eph. 1:4). God formulated the plan that includes each of us. And he's not making any pencil changes. Somehow, despite our doing things wrong and stupidly, God's blueprint remains unchanged.

2. *God's plan is loving.* We can perceive God's love around us in the world he has created. Many people can quickly acknowledge his loving plan for humanity. Those same folks quote verses such as "For God so loved the world." They readily acknowledge that God loves people. But the fact that he loves *them* specifically—that's hard for some to accept.

The Old Testament tells that Moses invited his father-in-law to join the Israelites on their trip out of Egypt into the promised land. He said, "Come with us and we will do you good." That's the operational plan of God. He always works toward making us better, healthier, and happier.

Our Father has no great need or desire to punish us. He's not out to trick us, trip us up, or catch us.

In the Old Testament we read of God punishing his people, and some portions sound awful. But the stories never *begin* with the chastisement. They start with God's pleading with the people through his prophets, begging them to return to him. Only afterwards does he say, "I'm wearied with you. You haven't repented; now you'll have to endure the consequences."

3. *God's guidance always brings glory to himself.* When God wills an event to happen, it's going to be good. People will recognize a little more of the greatness of God himself.

I've been pastor of the Riverdale Presbyterian Church for five years. One thing that keeps me excited about serving the Lord in this particular congregation is the spiritual growth. I can look at almost any phase of our congregational life—the sharing groups, the prayer fellowships, the choir, the youth. Adult classes that didn't even exist five years ago are now filled with people. Looking over the leadership of our congregation, I realize many of them weren't even members when I first came. Others, who have been here a long time, have only recently moved into their leadership positions. People are exercising their spiritual gifts, giving themselves to the life of the congregation.

And where does all this lead? It brings glory to God. I've heard more praising the Lord in the last two years than ever before. We're maturing, but we're also recognizing that God is the one carrying out the maturing process.

4. *God's guidance has our ultimate happiness in view.* I have to insert the word *ultimate*. That's the only way we can understand when God shouts "No!" Immediate circumstances may look as though our comfortable worlds have been bombarded with insurmountable forces. But that's only for the present. That's not the long view.

I remember, as a child, noticing how my mother took the hard knocks in life. She did her share of crying over problems, but I could always tell when she had worked through the pain and the self-pity. She'd go about her housework, singing "Farther Along":

> Farther along we'll know all about it,
> Farther along we'll understand why;
> Cheer up, my brother, live in the sunshine,
> We'll understand it all by and by.*

And she really believed the words of that song. She had the kind of faith that said, "Today's setbacks and tragedies, no matter how tough, are only temporary."

What's God's will for me?

When we look at our situations from an objective viewpoint, when we understand God's working principles, we can rejoice. Ultimately, there's only good ahead for us—because God is good. He only wants the best for his people, and his best means making them perfect.

---

*W.B. Stevens, in *Old Fashioned Revival Hour Songs* (Winona Lake, Ind.: Rodeheaver, Hall-Mack Co).

3.

You Really Can't Get There from Here

Perhaps you've heard the story of the city man who, after driving for hours in the country, admitted he was impossibly lost. He stopped a farmer who was plowing in a field and asked him for directions to reach the main road.

The farmer scratched his head and started giving directions. "Well, turn left at the crossroads, go six miles, and then—no, turn right at the crossroads, drive until you reach a fork in the road, and—no, you have to—why man, you can't reach the main road from here."

That old story says a lot about the realm of guidance. At times it seems we really can't get *there* from *here*. We know where we want to go, and we're all set to get there, but then we find that the way we plan to take is closed to us, or unforeseen developments take us in directions we never counted on.

A friend of mine took advantage of a special program offered by one of the big airlines—unlimited travel for about four hundred dollars. He visited fifteen major cities in three weeks. But he also had to pass through Atlanta five times in reaching those cities!

Our lives sometimes seem so much like that—they are full of detours, recrossings, seemingly endless delays. But they're not without purpose!

My friend Don helped me see this clearly. During a lunchtime conversation, Don mentioned that he had been previously married, divorced, and was now happily remarried.

I started to say how sorry I was, but Don stopped me. "Don't feel sorry. It was one of the best things that ever happened as far as my spiritual growth is concerned."

He went on to say that he had once been an extremely self-righteous person. He had spoken against Christians who couldn't work out their problems. "I used to say, 'If you'll pray together you'll solve your problems,' or 'Just stick with it; everything will work out.' Then I'd imply that if they really trusted God, he wouldn't let their problems overwhelm them.'"

Don smiled at me and said, "Then it happened to me. My whole life fell into a hundred pieces. I don't think I could ever have been tolerant or understanding about people's failures, because I'd never been there. Now, when I hear about another person's problems in marriage, or business, or any other aspect of life, I am a lot more compassionate. I had to fall on my face to learn to feel with other people."

I've wondered if the apostle Peter wasn't a bit like that too. I've always felt that it was necessary for him to go through a number of humbling experiences before God could use him to his fullest capacity.

Peter was always getting in trouble because of his rash words and actions. He was rebuked by Jesus for wanting to build shrines on the mountain where Jesus was transfigured. (I assume this was a way of trying to hold on to a momentary spiritual experience.) He went through the humiliation of denying his Lord after declaring, "Jesus, I'll never let you down." He was even admonished by the apostle Paul for his fickleness in eating with Gentiles when no Jews were around, but deserting them as soon as Jews appeared (see Gal. 2).

Before Peter could fulfill the purpose God had for him, he had to grow up. His detours, his stumblings, were necessary for his maturity in the faith. He couldn't go straight into perfection. He had to go somewhere else first.

I think that's often the way God leads his people. Through reflecting on my own experiences and those of other Christians, I've learned to recognize that following God's will doesn't always mean traveling in a straight line. The Lord actually leads us into detours, sidepaths, and circuitous trips. But he does it with a purpose—to get us where he wants us to go. He can see—even when we sometimes can't—that often the more indirect route is the more apt to get us to our destination. And he very often has things that need to be done along the way.

The life of the apostle Paul illustrates this principle. Almost immediately after the man's conversion at Damascus, the Holy Spirit spoke to Ananias and predicted that Paul would speak before royalty: "He is a chosen instrument of mine to carry my name before the Gentiles and kings and the sons of Israel" (Acts 9:15).

Eventually Paul *did* speak before royalty. But first he made several missionary journeys. He languished inside many prisons and suffered the pain of beatings; many times his persecutors stoned him. He constantly faced threats of death. It was after many years of service that he finally appeared before King Agrippa, and later went to Rome itself.

An incident in the life of Jesus shows us more about this subject. Jesus had been ministering in the area around Jerusalem (according to John's Gospel), and then headed toward Cana of Galilee—mentioned at the end of chapter four. John 4:4 reads, "He had to pass through Samaria."

That seemingly simple statement raises some questions when we realize that there were several ways to get from Jerusalem to Cana *without* going through Samaria. Jesus could have taken the road which followed the seacoast, or the one which wound through Perea. The road Jesus took, although actually the shortest, was the one least used by the Jews, because of deep prejudices between Jews and Samaritans. The average Jew would consider the trip through Samaria an unpleasant detour.

So why does the Gospel say Jesus "had to" go that way? The verb translated "had to" (in the King James Version, "must needs go through") may have meant that Jesus wanted to save time and physical exertion. However, looking at other passages in John's Gospel in which the Lord stressed his reliance upon the Father's directions may suggest another interpretation (see 2:4, 7:30, 8:20, 12:23, 13:1, 11:31). These other passages, along with the immediate context (see 4:1–3), lead us to believe that Jesus went through Samaria for one reason: God sent him.

24

Galilee may have been the next destination for the disciples and for Jesus, but God wanted the stopover in Samaria. And, while there, Jesus ministered to a needy woman. As the Lord sat at the well, the woman came to draw water. He taught her about God. And through her the entire village came out to hear Jesus speak.

Had Jesus gone a different way, he would never have had the opportunity to share God's love with that fallen woman of Samaria. She, in turn, would never have told the entire village about Jesus. They would never have cried out, "We believe."

And it all happened because Jesus *had to* go through Samaria on his way to Galilee. He had to go because God led him that way.

I firmly believe that nothing in our lives happens by accident, that God uses everything, no matter how seemingly insignificant, by putting it into the plan for our growth. Often we can look back at our bad moves, our unwise decisions, our unfortunate circumstances, and see how God used those in guiding us toward spiritual maturity or in accomplishing his overall plan.

Even the first Christians had to learn that through experience. The early chapters of the book of Acts contain stories of healing, deliverance from evil spirits, great miracles. In two days of preaching, four thousand people were converted. How the word multiplied in the city of Jerusalem!

Then, in the midst of all the shouting and the multiplying of converts and the healing of diseases, the game plan changed. "And on that day a great persecution arose against the church in Jerusalem; and they were all scattered throughout the region of Judea and Samaria, except the apostles" (Acts 8:1).

I'm sure many of those disciples looked upon this event as tragic. Perhaps they even saw it as the end of the great Christian kingdom in Jerusalem. But we know that Jesus had given them a command on the day of his ascension: "You shall be my witnesses in Jerusalem and in all Judea and Samaria and to the end of the earth" (Acts 1:8).

It was part of his plan for them to spread the good news and not to keep it in only one city. Philip went to a city of Samaria

(Acts 8:4–40) and fulfilled one portion of the command. Others spread the news to more distant places. At Damascus, the great Apostle had his conversion experience—and a disciple named Ananias was there, waiting for God to use him!

I haven't always been able to look at circumstances and say, "This is the way the Lord has led me," but I'm learning. I'm at least learning that my spiritual growth isn't always in one predictable direction.

It's not a matter of climbing one spiritual mountain after another. In between mountain peaks I encounter pitfalls, detours, backtracking, rerouting. But I know that God doesn't waste his guidance. I may not be able to get there from here—at least not directly—but I am secure knowing that, even if I have to go to three or four other places first, I'm eventually going to reach my destination.

4.

Don't Do Something

"When did you first feel God wanted you in the ministry?" a friend asked. I had trouble answering that question. I don't really know *when.*

I had one of those gradual conversion experiences, one which took place over a period of months. In September I began reading the Bible, visiting churches, and praying (even when I wasn't sure anyone was out there to hear me). By the following May, I could say, "I believe in Jesus Christ."

Almost from the moment I could speak of my commitment to Christ, I could also testify of my call to the ministry. The sense of that call has never really left me. After my military days and college, I taught in both public and parochial schools, but I always knew these positions were temporary—steps along the way until the Lord placed me in full-time Christian ministry.

From the time of my conversion, I've wanted to work for the Lord. Great portions of my time with the Lord have centered around the question, "What do you want me to do, Lord?" In fact, I have often identified myself by the particular phase of ministry in which I am engaged. At one time I would say, "I'm a missionary." Today at writers' conferences it sometimes comes out, "I'm a Christian writer." Most often I describe myself as a pastor or a gospel minister. In all these instances I identify myself as a Christian by what I *do* for the Lord.

Much of my life has been built on *doing* for Christ. And much of my concern for guidance has centered around getting directions for the next activity. There's nothing wrong with that orientation, but lately I have begun thinking of the Christian life and of divine guidance a little differently. I've shifted enough to see it this way: God calls us first to *be*, then to *do*.

I'm not merely attempting to play with words. If we grasp the principle that being, not doing, should come first in terms of both time and importance, we will be able to keep our lives and our activities straight. Reversing the order often brings us trouble.

The Old Testament records an account of a runner, Ahima-az, who wanted to deliver an up-to-the-last-arrow account of the battles between King David's troops and those of the rebellious Absalom. Commander Joab sent a Cushite instead, but Ahima-az still wanted to run. Joab asked, "Why will you run, my son?" The would-be messenger didn't answer, but persisted in his request until, finally, Joab granted permission. Ahima-az ran across the plains, overtook the Cushite, and reached King David first. Then, either because he didn't know the outcome of the battle, or perhaps because he was afraid to tell of Absalom's death, he merely said, "All is well."

Then David's watchman saw the Cushite coming, and Ahima-az stepped aside until the real messenger arrived and gave the complete message (see 2 Sam. 18:19–33).

That's the story: Ahima-az ran, but he didn't have a real message to carry. He only wanted to run. I've often been like that man—ready for action—and, like Ahima-az, I've not always been sent. Yet, in my eagerness to serve, I ran on.

It probably has something to do with my nature. I'm the activist type. I'd rather be doing something—anything—than just sitting still. I'm sure that's also true for others. We're so busy doing that we have little time to be.

That's probably why Paul wrote so much in Galatians and Romans (and in other places) against earning our salvation. Our relationship to Jesus Christ is based on *God's activity*, not ours. We receive; he gives. As far as we're concerned, it's a passive activity.

We're always trying to turn things around the other way. It's almost as though we try to say, "Lord, I work for you, so you have to accept me." We even tend to look at other people in terms of what they accomplish. Perhaps the following three experiences will clarify what I mean:

After graduating from an Atlanta seminary, Dan received a call as pastor of a Louisiana church. He was installed as pastor; then, one month after his ordination, a head-on automobile collision took his life.

Senia and her husband, Hayden, started home from church one night with their infant daughter in the back seat of the car. They were making plans to go as missionaries to South America. As Hayden drove home, he obeyed the octagonal sign and stopped, but a drunken teen-age driver didn't. The collision killed Senia instantly, leaving the distraught father to raise a small child alone.

The New Testament book of Acts portrays Stephen as one of the most promising leaders of the early church. He started by waiting on tables and serving food to Greek widows. He soon became a powerful voice in the Jerusalem church and a mighty preacher. He preached a magnificent sermon, which is recorded in Acts 7, but he never quite finished that message; fanatical Jews stoned him while he was still preaching.

When we hear stories like these, we tend to think, "What a pity. They all showed such promise. How much they might have *accomplished* for the cause of Christ if only they had lived!"

Paul is constantly held up as the greatest of the apostles. Why do we laud him by that title? We judge largely on the basis of what we know through the New Testament record—that Paul was a man of accomplishment. Paul dominates the book of Acts. We have more than a dozen of his letters left for us to read. Because Paul *did* so much, we think of him as the greatest apostle. But perhaps Philip the evangelist, or Peter, or one of the others—perhaps Stephen—deserves that title, for different reasons. Does accomplishment have to be the sole criterion for worth?

Our preoccupation with action and accomplishment extends to our books, our sermons, our conversations—even our hymns. As I skimmed through two hymnals I jotted down the titles and messages of hymns in the sections called "God's Will" and "Guidance."

Most of the guidance hymns are action songs! "Where He

Leads Me I Will Follow" comes next to "Lead On, O King Eternal." "Jesus, Savior, Pilot Me" lies across the page from "He Leadeth Me! O Blessed Tho't." A few pages later, one of my favorites appears: "Guide Me, O Thou Great Jehovah." The second hymnal offers, in addition, "All the Way My Savior Leads Me." Another hymn starts out, "Jesus, I my cross have taken, / All to leave, and follow Thee . . ."

We need active-type songs like these. But perhaps the guidance sections of our hymnbooks also need to include songs with themes such as:

> Be still, my soul: The Lord is on thy side;
> Bear patiently the cross of grief or pain;
> Leave to thy God to order and provide;
> In every change He faithful will remain.*

Or how about "I am Thine, O Lord?" "Just as I am" may be a better expression of the guidance relationship than an evangelistic piece.

I'm appreciating more and more the importance of being—simply being—God's person. If I am his person, then I'll obey him. If I'm his, then he'll guide my activities. I'm convinced that my first responsibility in the realm of guidance is to learn when *not* to do something. I commit myself to God, then I wait for orders to move.

We can say this in several other ways. We need to be receivers before we can be givers. We need to be God's recruits before we can be his marching army.

Remember the story of Paul's conversion experience? God struck down the fiery Pharisee as he traveled the Damascus road. Paul's question was, "Who are you, Lord?" (Acts 9:5). From there, men led him into the city, where he stayed in a house for three days. The great ministry of the apostle then unfolds in the succeeding chapters.

Had it been most of us on the road to Damascus, I imagine

---

*Katharina von Schlegel, tr. Jane Laurie Bothwick, in *The Hymnbook* (Philadelphia: Westminster Press, 1955).

our question would have been, "Lord, what do you want me to *do?*" We'd rather jump into action than define our relationship. However, somewhere in our growing commitment to Jesus Christ we need to settle the question of being versus doing.

While pondering that question, a phrase from an old love song filtered through my mind: "I'm yours to command." That's the place to start.

I'm yours, God. I'm here. Activities grow out of that. But we start with simply acknowledging who we are and who God is.

A newspaper item I read recently told of a wealthy man who owns homes in California, New York, and Florida. He keeps each home fully staffed. Employees must be ready on three hours' notice to provide total service, including a full-course meal. For the employees of the house in Florida, which he visited less than three weeks last year, this means days and weeks of simply being there, staying ready for action at his command.

As we think of the realm of guidance we need to realize that *presence* precedes *guidance*. God wants to direct our lives and make them useful. But they have to be his first.

I saw this illustrated recently with my young grandson Danny. He's one of those children who jumps out of bed and bounces all day long, never napping, and then slowly unwinds at night when he heads for bed. One day, while visiting us, he played outside for awhile, then pulled, pushed, or threw everything movable, and played with every toy in our house. All this time I was reclining in an easy chair, reading. Finally, Danny hopped into the chair next to me. I expected him to tickle or punch me, but he merely snuggled close and put his head on my shoulder.

"What do you want, Danny?"

"Nothin'. I just want to be with you."

For several minutes he lay against me, scarcely moving. I gently hugged him. Then he said, "Grampa, will you play with me now?"

How could I refuse that request? As I thought of the incident it became clear that's how God wants us. First, we draw closer to him, rest in him, be aware of his presence. Then we can ask, "Father, will you go with me now?"

How can God refuse?

31

5.

Who Switched the Sign?

One evening, while in the process of visiting church prospects, I looked for a street called Heather Lane. Knowing its approximate location, I drove along until I saw the sign for the street, then turned. But the numbers didn't match the address I wanted. I drove up and down the full length of the street for ten minutes. Finally it hit me—I wasn't on Heather Lane at all; I was on Collingswood! Somebody—probably as a joke—had turned the sign around, and it was facing the wrong direction. No wonder I couldn't find the house; I had been on the wrong street all along.

Shortly after that experience, a book salesman told me of something that had happened to him in the Midwest. He had stopped at a Christian bookstore to make a sale and had discovered it was closed. A sign hung in the window:

On January 2, 1978, God led me into this ministry.
On September 30, 1979, God led me out of this ministry.

My friend mused, "The Lord might have led the man out, but he went out through the door of bankruptcy. He also cheated our company out of three thousand dollars as the Spirit led him out."

Thinking of those two incidents raises some questions about guidance. My going the wrong way at Collingswood and Heather was a natural mistake. I followed the green sign with white letters, having no way of knowing it pointed in the wrong direction. But what about the bookstore owner? Surely he went into business after asking God's directions. He must have felt an affirmative nod, and then acted accordingly. Does God lead a person to open a Christian bookstore (or any other kind of business), and then close two years later out of financial strain? If the man read the sign correctly the first time—and he still declared that God had led him into the business—who switched the sign?

Several possibilities come to mind.

1. *He may have simply misread the sign.* Recently I checked a street map of Atlanta and found fifty-eight different streets, all bearing the word, *Peachtree.* In that city you can't simply say "Peachtree" and be sure of ending up in the right place. You have to say "Peachtree Road" or "Peachtree Battle" or "Peach-tree Creek." To get where you want to go, you have to read the whole sign.

That's also true in the realm of divine guidance. Sometimes we have problems because we stop "reading" God's signs too soon. I think that's what happened to Bob.

Bob owned a small business, and it had begun to prosper. One day he said to his pastor, "I've been praying about it, and I believe God wants me to buy a new car." Until that time, Bob had never had much success in any venture. He always drove old cars that required more funds for maintenance than the cars were worth.

Bob bought the car—a Lincoln Continental. Shortly afterwards the business reversed itself, and Bob had to scrape to meet his payments.

His pastor told me, "In Bob's prayers and conversations after that, I sensed that he expected God to send in customers so he could make car payments, along with taking care of his other indebtedness. His attitude almost suggested that *God* owned the car."

As I listened, I thought perhaps God *had* wanted Bob to buy a new car—but a four-cylinder model without air conditioning, AM-FM radio, cruise control, and CB equipment. Perhaps Bob wanted a really impressive car so badly that he read the message incorrectly.

2. *God may have led, but the man failed.* During the years my wife and I spent as missionaries in Africa, we met dozens of new recruits. They all came to serve Jesus Christ. One couple went home within a year. Another stayed three, but probably should have gone back after six months.

Yet each of them, when they first touched African soil, said, "God called me." I wouldn't have argued. God may have called, but perhaps they failed in what he called them to do.

One couple who left midway through their first year simply could not adjust to the African culture. The husband, for instance, didn't like the nationals walking in front of his house (even though they had always done it). He carefully marked off and dug out a narrow path for them to use. But the natives, used to walking where they chose in their own country, and unused to fences, continued as before. They couldn't understand why they should have to walk an extra three hundred feet when they could just as easily cut in front of his house.

At one point, the man actually stood in front of his house and threw rocks at the people!

The couple who left after three discouraging years might have made it except for serious character flaws—again those of the husband. In his dictatorial manner, he made pronouncements, and expected the Africans to carry them out. He continually berated them, and frequently complained, "I came here to serve you, to show you the way to God, and see how you ignore my teachings!"

3. *He may have raced ahead of God.* Remember the story of Joseph in the Old Testament? The young man had visions, and a dream that his brothers would bow before him. He knew of his eventual exaltation. That happened, of course—thirty years later. But instead of holding the revelations in his heart, he taunted his brothers with his dreams. He earned much of their scorn.

Racing ahead of God has been a problem for me many times. Once, during our days in Africa, we felt we ought to make a change. We lived on a mission compound in a remote part of western Kenya. Much of my work could have been done by the Africans themselves, and I felt they were ready for the leadership. I often argued, "Why don't we missionaries move into places where the nationals still need us, and leave them the jobs they can do for themselves?" I prayed about the move for several weeks. One day I knew the Lord had heard me and had given me a "Yes." The next day we started packing.

We moved on—eighteen months later!

I had been right in praying. The Lord had spoken. But I hadn't heard the Lord's timing. We could have saved ourselves both frustration and embarrassment, had we only waited until the Lord said, "Now."

4. *The man may not have wanted to read the sign correctly.* At times we all get our own desires mixed up with God's will. Something pulls us strongly. We want to buy a house, a microwave oven, or an organ. We want to change jobs, or move to the country. Our desires grow so strong, we have difficulty hearing God's voice.

That's exactly the experience of a newly divorced woman I know. Lydia says, "I should never have married Lyle in the first place. I knew within a week after the wedding, but it was too late then." She talks about their courtship; Lyle had represented everything the American girl wants. He was the rising executive with a progressive company, already making a good salary. Physically he was quite a catch; Lyle could easily have modeled men's clothing. He loved children, and treated Lydia kindly. "But," she admitted, "it just didn't work out for us. He never wanted to go anyplace. He wouldn't talk. When he did talk, he expected me to answer him like his personal slave."

Lydia confessed that, prior to the wedding, as the big day grew closer, doubts crept in. Instead of asking God's will, she kept saying, "Oh, it happens to everyone." She also admitted she was afraid to pray—afraid that God might not let her marry Lyle.

"Looking back," she said, "I can see that God tried several times to show me we were not right for each other. But I didn't want to understand his message. In fact, a few times I even said to friends, 'The devil is working overtime to confuse me.' They all agreed! After all, Lyle and I looked like the ideal couple."

Lydia's experience reminds me of James 4:2, "You do not have, because you do not ask." The next verse reads: "You ask and do not receive, because you ask wrongly, to spend it on your passions."

God's guidance comes for us to follow, not to bend to our plans.

Who switched the sign? I'll never know who turned it around at Heather and Collingswood. For me, the incident had only minor consequences. But what about the bookstore owner? I've wondered a lot about him.

Of course, the Holy Spirit may have led him into business and then back out in less than two years. But I find it incredible to believe that God led him so specifically without leading him to take care of his bills, or at least to arrange for payment.

What about the man *now?* He failed in business. He failed in two years of his life. How does he feel about it? I hope he doesn't blame God. I hope he doesn't cry out, "Lord, I did what you said—and now look! I've lost everything, and I was trying to serve you."

I hope he can say, "I misread the sign," or "The sign had the right message, but I failed." I hope the man will read signs more carefully in the future. God wants to guide. He promises that. But we have to do it his way.

Who switched the sign?

I know it wasn't God!

And maybe it's time to forget about that sign. It's enough to know that making a few mistakes doesn't wipe us out forever. We belong to a God who forgives mistakes, even when the signs get turned around.

6.

Getting It Perfect

"I always follow God's perfect will, because I always obey him perfectly," Gus said.

Those words, on paper at least, sound boastful. But that's not the way Gus spoke them. He spoke in a humble, almost self-effacing manner.

I'm not sure Gus always received perfect guidance from the Lord, but I know he sought it. Whenever decisions came up— and some of them were extremely small—he prayed. He wanted the Lord to show him exactly what to do, how to do it, and when.

Most of us may not spend as much time in prayer for guidance as Gus—he spent hours every day at this—but our desire can be as real. Most of us, when we make a commitment of our lives to Christ, say, "Yes, I want God to lead me totally."

The problem is, we don't get that perfect guidance. At least, not all the time. We pray. We seek for God to show us. But we don't always have clear-cut revelations out of heaven. Flashing lights of insight don't hit us every day. Money doesn't drop into our hands. Circumstances don't change drastically.

The fact is that none of us is sure of God's will 100 percent of the time. We hear from God; we try to obey; then we find ourselves reaching for more light and for greater understanding.

There is a reason why our reach is always short of perfect— we're not! From a theological viewpoint, we make the same confession when we acknowledge that we're all sinners. The very

37

fact of the sinful impulse working in all of us is enough to prevent a full revelation of God's will in our lives. I can pull out dozens of verses to prove my point, such as these in the third chapter of Romans:

"All have turned aside, together they have gone wrong" (v. 12).

"None is righteous, no, not one" (v. 10).

"No one understands, no one seeks for God" (v. 11).

"All have turned aside, together they have gone wrong" (v. 12).

"No one does good, not even one" (v. 12).

"All have sinned and fall short of the glory of God" (v. 23).

That doesn't mean that we need to despair. But understanding our sinful condition does offer us comfort when we fail. It helps us grapple with the fact of our own inherent sinfulness, our lack of perfect communion with a perfect God.

I'm convinced that through each year of my Christian experience I grow a little more. Each year I understand more and respond better to God's guidance. But, at the same time, I never quite make it. None of us does.

As I worked on this chapter, one of the women in our church came in. She wore a gold chain of half-inch gold letters spelling the single word *perfect*. The only problem is, the letter *T* was slanted! That's about the way perfection works for us, isn't it? We almost make it—but there's always at least one crooked letter marring our perfection.

In the same way, guidance is less than perfect for us. It's the sin factor working in our lives that makes the difference. And being sinful is simply part of being human.

It's important to be aware of that when we pray for guidance. For one thing, it helps us rethink our motives, to consider why we want what we want. For instance, do we pray for an increase in pay so we can give more to God, or to provide better living standards for our families? Or do we want money for more selfish reasons?

One time, while I was a member of a small church, problems

broke out and we barely averted a split. During that period I had been misquoted and misunderstood. I prayed for the situation to be righted. As I continued to bombard heaven to get it all straightened out, I finally had to admit that I wanted vindication rather than merely having the situation cleared up. That was sin at work in my life; I was praying for the right thing, but with the wrong motives.

Acknowledging the sinfulness of our natures also helps us in thinking about our attitudes. In a church of which I was pastor, one woman constantly criticized me and made life quite painful. I frequently prayed for the Lord to set her straight. I didn't really want God's love to enfold the woman; I didn't even pray for her to grow in her faith; I just wanted to be rid of her. I also wanted to see her punished for all her wrongdoing.

After weeks of praying (and finally re-examining my own attitude), I finally saw what God had intended for me to realize all along—that she was a child of God, badly in need of love and understanding.

Once I accepted the sinfulness of my attitude, I could work with her. We never became friends, but at least I could say I grew to love her and to care about what happened to her.

As long as we're human and capable of sin, we'll never have perfect guidance. But there are ways in which God does guide us.

In later chapters I'll be writing specifically about each of the means of guidance. For this section, I briefly suggest some of the ways that I use to ascertain God's guidance.

1. *The most obvious: praying.* I pray, and I expect God to speak to my inner thoughts, giving me a sense of direction.

2. *Reading the Bible.* As I've read, at times God has made a portion of the Bible so meaningful to me that his will was clear.

3. *At other times, sharing the dilemma with a friend or a small group is helpful.* Their counsel has often been God's way of showing his will to me.

There was a time, after we had been in Kenya as missionaries nearly five straight years, when I felt physically drained and emotionally dried up. I kept getting sick with things like colds and other minor illnesses that never really kept me down, but which kept me from functioning at my best. I seemed always to be getting over one illness or just starting a new one.

I asked friends for prayers. One courageous sister said, "I'll pray for you, Cec, but I already know the answer. You've overextended yourself. You're not taking care of your body and getting enough sleep. You need to take at least a week's vacation—it'll do wonders for you."

She was right. I followed her advice, slept ten to twelve hours at a stretch. Within a week, I felt great. Her words were God's wisdom to me.

4. *Listening to circumstances* aids me in knowing God's will. My wife Shirley's career evolved out of just the simple flow of circumstances.

When I first began writing, an Atlanta publisher looked at some of my material. Even though he rejected it, he commented, "The typing is absolutely excellent. Do you type your own work?"

"No," I replied, "my wife does it."

"If she's interested in typing for us, have her give us a call."

Our children were all in school. Shirley was not working, and was getting a little bored at home. She went to work as a typist— three days a week. Soon they asked her to work full time. One day her boss quit without giving notice. The president asked my wife, "Will you fill in until we can find someone else?"

Two weeks later he said to Shirley, "You've done so well, I've decided to stop looking, if you'll take the job." She did!

That's another way the Lord works—through the circumstances in our lives. Shirley took the typing job to give herself something to do and to bring in extra income. She moved into the next position because it seemed the logical thing to do in the situation.

5. This leads to one other means of determining God's leading. *He allows us to use our common sense.* If my wastebasket's on fire, I don't have to pray, "Lord, should I put out the fire?" I rush at it and get the fire out!

I know a man who prays each time he gets his paycheck. He asks, "Should I pay this bill, Lord?" He holds each bill in his hands, pauses for guidance, and then either writes the check or goes on to the next.

When he told me that, I said, "Jack, you don't need to pray about that! You owe money, if you've got the money to pay it—then pay."

"But I want to be sure of God's will—"

"Jack, doesn't Romans 13:8 say to owe no man anything? If you owe, pay. You don't need to ask God."

I spoke a bit harshly to Jack, but I felt he was asking God to do what God expected him to do for himself. If money had been tight (it wasn't in this case), I could understand how Jack might pray, "Lord, I have only seventy-five dollars, and the bills total to over two hundred dollars. Help me to know how to slice up the funds."

While we never get it perfect in our search for guidance, we keep moving ahead. We keep praying. We continue searching our hearts and looking for more perfect means of knowing God's will. And that always honors him.

I remember when my son was finishing first grade. The school sponsored a field day; all the children competed in events such as broad jump, races, and high jump. My young son competed in every event, running or jumping as best he could. Being the youngest as well as the smallest child in the school, he naturally won nothing. But he kept trying. The results, compared to the others, seemed so pitiful. But to young John Mark, they were the best he could do.

I remember seeing the disappointed look on his face each time the school principal announced the winners and his name wasn't among them. He couldn't understand; he didn't have the maturity to realize how badly he had competed against the others. "I tried, Daddy. I tried," he kept saying.

"Yes, son, you kept trying," I answered as I hugged him. "And that makes me so proud of you."

Perhaps spiritual guidance is like that, too. The difference is that we don't compete against anyone else. Maybe we don't run a perfect race, but we can give our all to the effort. And that's what God considers.

7.

Infallible Guidance

Janie always believed in using the Bible for guidance from the Lord. Whenever a question arose, she would pray. Then, with eyes still closed, she would flip open her Bible, stab a spot with her finger, and open her eyes. For Janie, that was always the guidance from the Lord—even when she never quite understood what it was saying to her.

I wouldn't want to say that the Holy Spirit never guides that way. I would never want to preclude God's sovereign right to speak in any way he chooses.

In fact, one of my most significant experiences of receiving a word from the Lord fits into that kind of an experience. I didn't close my eyes and poke my finger on a page. But I did open my Bible one day at random.

It happened in 1963, while I was a missionary in Kenya, East Africa. Everything had been moving smoothly as far as the progress of my work was concerned, but my relationship with the Africans had not gone well. No matter how hard I tried, they seemed always against me. Later, I learned that one of their leaders had spread vicious stories about me.

One morning, weary and almost at the point of giving up, I opened my Weymouth New Testament, deciding to read, but not even sure where to read. It fell open at Acts 28:2: "The natives showed us remarkable kindness. . . ."

Immediately I knew that was the Holy Spirit speaking to me, encouraging me—a promise that God would turn the Africans to think favorably toward me. Within a year, my whole relationship had changed, and many intimate friendships had developed.

That happened *once* in my life as a Christian. It might happen again. I wouldn't want to say God can't or won't work that way. But it's not his *usual* method of directing his people.

Before going into how we receive guidance from the Bible, let's pause to emphasize the purpose of the sacred book. This inspired collection of writings isn't written as a story of history, or as a science text. Essentially, the Bible records the story of God's people and his dealings with them. It's a spiritual record, from the beginnings of time through the first century.

And yet, it's a timeless book, because the author operates in the world today. The Holy Spirit who inspired the scribes to put down the messages contained in the Bible's sixty-six books is the same Spirit who is with us today. He continues to guide the church and the individuals in it, and he uses the Bible for that purpose. But giving specific guidance to God's people is *not* the Bible's first purpose!

Recently I heard a radio preacher talk about the Bible, and he said something like this: "Here's God's Word to guide you. Every answer is here for you. Every problem's solution is found within the pages of this wonderful book."

His statements bothered me. I both agreed and disagreed with what he said. If he meant that every specific problem has a specific answer, I'm ready to shout, "No!" But if he meant God has drawn guidelines and shown principles in the Bible, that the Holy Spirit takes these broad statements and applies them to modern situations, then I agree.

For instance, we have situations in our modern world that the biblical folks never dreamed about. The Bible makes no direct reference to moral issues such as genetic engineering, organ transplants, artificial insemination. One reason we have such a polarity on the abortion issue in the church today certainly is the fact that we find no specific passage which categorically states a position on the issue. Both sides of the controversy base their arguments on inferences, on theological understandings, and on broad principles, but not on specific verses.

At the same time, the Bible speaks specifically to problems of the day and culture in which it was written, issues which may seem foreign to us. Moses settled the question of whether women could own property in his day and, after going into the promised land, Caleb reinforced it. Paul stated categorically that women should wear veils in public because he faced a serious problem in the Corinthian church. He also intervened in the problem of whether it was right to buy meat that had previously been offered in sacrifice to idols.

How, then, do we go about receiving guidance from the Bible about the problems and issues that concern us? First, I believe we need to distinguish which portions are intended for eternal guidance. Which specific passages does God intend for us to observe perpetually? Most of them are rather obvious—injunctions against murder, idolatry, adultery, covetousness, and jealousy.

Second, we need to read for the eternal *principles* in the Bible—principles upon which we need to think in making our decisions. That means the commandments about loving God with all our hearts. Paul exhorts us to live peacefully with all people, so far as it depends on us. We're called blessed if we're peacemakers and if we don't seek revenge. All these are timeless words from God.

Who of us argues today over whether we can buy and eat meat sacrificed in the temples? That's absolutely foreign to our culture. Yet, we can take a passage such as that dealing with meat in 1 Corinthians and extrapolate principles for guidance.

One of them would go like this: if any action or activity of mine, even one in which I personally see no harm, confuses a weaker Christian or causes him to stumble, I need to re-examine my activity. Perhaps I ought to leave it alone, rather than hinder another person's spiritual growth.

When I say that the Bible speaks to some specific cultural issues that do not apply to us, I'm not trying to bury it in the dark ages. The Bible still speaks to us today. We can gain positive helps on guidance—once we understand what we're trying to do.

Here are a few ideas:

1. *Read the Bible on a systematic basis.* As we know more about God's Word, we learn more about God. We begin understanding how the Holy Spirit works in the lives of people. We understand how God speaks. We perceive more of the divine principles upon which he operates.

I saw this clearly during my military days. For two years I worked under Lieutenant Commander DeLay—a conscientious, hard-working man. He was in charge of court martial reviews, and I was the number one enlisted man on his staff. During my two years of serving under him, I learned to sense what he'd say, how he'd say certain things, and how he'd react in various situations.

By the time we had worked together a few months, I could hear the first sentence or two of his statements and often fill in the rest. After I had been with Commander DeLay a year, he also realized this. He would often write little notes, two or three lines long, and give them to me. From his notes I would then type up complete, two-page statements. I could do it because I understood what he wanted and how his mind operated.

That's partially how I understand my relationship with Jesus Christ. The more I read my Bible, the more I gain an understanding of the divine mind. I perceive more accurately how the Holy Spirit operates in our lives.

For example, I'm not comfortable in buying lottery tickets or involving myself in any kind of chances to win from a slot machine, drawing, or bingo. While I can give no direct biblical references, and I'm not setting myself up as opposing those who can indulge, I hesitate, because in my understanding gambling is not congruent with God's plan for me.

2. *Don't merely jump into the middle of the Bible.* Allow God to impress upon the mind what you've *already* read or memorized. Psalm 119:11 says, "I have laid up thy word in my heart, that I might not sin against thee."

For me, that makes a good case for memorizing portions of the Bible, allowing its words to sink into our subconscious minds. Then, in God's time and during particular circumstances, the words and meanings come to the surface. Paul tells us that *all* Scripture is profitable. Even if we don't memorize, a frequent reading and hearing makes many scriptures come alive in our thoughts at the needed moment.

One Sunday, at the conclusion of a worship service, one man started telling me how angry he was over the way I prayed. "You didn't say 'Thee' Or 'Thou' once—not once—in addressing God."

As he ranted on, I silently asked God what to do, how to answer the man. A verse came to mind: "Answer not a fool according to his folly, lest you be like him yourself" (Prov. 26:4). I then mumbled something about being sorry he felt that way.

A few days later, the man called me on the phone. "I acted like a fool. I'm sorry."

I'm convinced that the Holy Spirit put that verse in my mind for that appropriate moment, to help me keep from responding in anger.

3. Measure your experience with that of God's saints. Realizing how they acted and reacted in situations can guide us in our lives.

One time in Africa, thieves broke into our house in the middle of the night, intending to rob us, even to kill us if necessary. However, due to the intervention of local Africans, they didn't harm us. They ran off, afraid and empty-handed.

Afterwards, the District Officer suggested that I apply for a gun permit and then buy a gun, "in case of another attempt."

I obtained the permit, but when it came to actually buying a gun, I couldn't do it. Part of my decision came from the fact that I simply could not shoot another human being. But the other part of my decision rested upon a principle I understood from the story of Ezra.

King Artaxerxes sent Ezra back to rebuild Jerusalem after the exile. The king offered to send troops with the man of God to protect him, but Ezra refused them. Ezra writes,

> For I was ashamed to ask the king for a band of soldiers and horsemen to protect us against the enemy on our way; since we had told the king, "The hand of our God is for good upon all that

seek him, and the power of his wrath is against all that forsake him" (Ezra 8:22).

Like the priest Ezra, I had witnessed God's protection in my life; now was my chance to live by my faith. The robbers never returned to our mission, although the fact that they might was a constant source of concern. And we had taken our stand—we'd let the Lord become our protector.

We're always looking for infallible guides. And while I believe the Bible is infallible, that's not enough. We have the Book, but we also need to know how to use the Book.

And we need the Spirit that inspired the writers. We can't merely open the Book and exclaim, "Ah, here's God's will." But as the Holy Spirit makes its verses alive to us, we know we're being guided infallibly.

8.

It'll Cost You!

A friend fretted and groaned over an impending decision.

I finally asked, "Have you asked the Lord to show you what to do?"

"Certainly not!" she snapped back. "I'm afraid he'd tell me to do something I don't want to do. Then I'd really be in a mess!"

Actually, she was kidding. But we sometimes try that with the Lord. We deliberately avoid seeking his direction. Perhaps we're not quite sure we want the right answer. Perhaps we want our own way so badly we don't want to hear the Holy Spirit.

We tend to decide what we want, work toward it, and then ask God to bless. We avoid really communicating with him about it. That way God won't thwart our plans.

We need to ask ourselves from time to time, "Do I really want God to lead me?" And before we answer that question, we need to remind ourselves that it'll cost us something if we give an affirmative reply.

It also costs us when we *don't* ask. When I was in my early teens, an event occurred in our town—the first of what we called "midnight shows." The featured film, one of those horror types, promised an intriguing story line, or so it seemed to me at that age. A headless man on horseback rode across the English moors at night, killing people.

I wanted to see the movie, and so did my friends. One way or another, all of them found a way to get permission to attend. I was sure that if I asked my dad, he'd laugh at anyone wanting to stay up that late. (The movie wouldn't end before two in the morning.) I was afraid he would forbid my going.

I decided to go anyway—and not ask! I reasoned, "I won't know what Dad will say if I don't ask him."

Naturally, I found out later—when I tried sneaking into the house at two forty-five in the morning. And I paid the consequences.

Not asking Dad's feelings on the matter didn't absolve me from blame!

I've seen this in adult behavior. I've talked to dozens of people whose marriages have gone on the rocks. One of them will often say something such as, "I knew it wasn't right to get married in the first place. But I loved him so much. I thought he would change."

Somewhere along the line we have to wake up. We have to face reality. Not always immediately, but eventually, we discover that we have to pay the price—the price of not obeying. We suffer the consequences of ignoring what God wants in our lives. That's the negative side of seeking guidance from the Holy Spirit.

On the positive side, there's the fact that when we do ask God, not only do we receive directions, but we are directed by One whose will always has as its goal our betterment and eventual happiness. We are also ensured against suffering the pangs of guilt and frustration afterwards.

We've said that if we want to know God's will it'll cost us. What does this mean?

One cost involved in knowing God's will involves *time*. We don't merely flip a switch, or dial a prayer. We may need a period of serious soul-searching and self-examination. That's often painful, and it can't always be done in an instant.

The Lord doesn't always respond with an immediate answer to our prayers. Sometimes we have to accept waiting until *he's* ready.

In the Old Testament, God told Elijah that it would not rain until the prophet said so. For three years, drought covered the land. One day the prophet prayed for rain, but no drops fell from heaven. He prayed again. Not a sprinkle. He kept on. Seven times he prayed before a raincloud, the size of a man's fist, appeared on the horizon. Then the rain came almost immediately.

That's often part of the price of receiving guidance from the Holy Spirit. We pray . . . and then we wait.

It doesn't matter what the question: Should I change jobs? Buy a house? Get a new car? The Lord cares about all areas of our lives, and he can—and will—guide us, if we allow him the time to speak.

The waiting can be like that of Elijah on the mountain. Even though he knew it would rain—he had that inner assurance—he had to continue praying until it happened.

Or there's the story of Hannah, who had no children. She prayed earnestly for the Lord to give her a son. Finally, after many years, the Lord told her that within a year she would conceive and bear a child—and she did.

Another cost involved in seeking God's will: *acknowledgment.*

That means saying, "I am not the master of my fate. I can't always work out my own problems. I need help."

I've discovered that for many people that's a tough place to stand. They easily thank God for creating the world, for loving us, even for sending a Savior. But to pray, "Lord, I can't do it myself. I can't handle this on my own"—that's hard. They're too used to thinking of themselves as self-sufficient.

This seems especially true of us men. We're often reluctant to accept the reality that at times we need help beyond ourselves. We all tumble into situations beyond our wisdom and capabilities. Not only do we need to acknowledge our inability to handle the crisis, but God wants us to go even further; he wants us also to admit that we are *his servants.*

A true servant waits for the master's command. But we keep wanting to do *our* will, then perhaps make allowances for God's intervention.

The New Testament keeps telling us that Jesus Christ purchased us at Calvary. His death was more than just a good deed; it gave him the ownership of us, his people.

So, if I'm really a Christian, I'm not my own person. I belong to Jesus Christ, no matter how repugnant that may sound to my sense of individualism.

When we acknowledge God's ownership, we acknowledge that God makes the choices because he knows what's best for us. He can look down the road and see the situations in advance.

His knowing what's best makes me think of parents and their young children. I suppose every child has moments of rebellion, often to learn that mother or father really did know best.

When I was a third grader, our school sponsored a fund-raising project. We sold flower seeds at a nominal cost, a portion of which went back to our school. I managed to unload my quota on neighbors. I also wanted my father to buy seeds and plant flowers. We had a large garden space, which he tilled every year.

Dad, being the practical kind, said, "You can't eat flowers. You put in a lot of work, look at them for awhile, and then they die."

I begged him to change his mind. I kept looking at the beautiful pictures of marigolds and zinnias on the package. Finally, I told him, "I've got money saved from my birthday. I'll buy the seeds and plant them and take care of them, too. Just show me a place to use."

My mother intervened. "It's a lot of hard work. You have to dig up the ground, and weed, and—"

"But I'll do it. I promise!"

My parents finally gave me a small section of the garden for my flowerbed. It took at least an hour to get the soil ready for planting. The result pleased me as I admired my six neat rows of seeds. Had the flowers bloomed during the first two weeks, I might have enjoyed success. But as the days grew warmer and the lure of play called me away from the house after school, I soon forgot about my marigolds and zinnias. I didn't even think about them again until midsummer. One morning I stopped to look. I saw one marigold—only one. Weeds completely covered the area I had planted. I never said anything to my parents. Years later, my mother said, "Dad and I knew what would happen, but you were so determined, so we let you have your own way."

That's like the workings of our heavenly Father. He's always trying to tell us what's best. But, like rebellious children, we're often so determined, we're not willing to listen.

One more thing about the cost of guidance: we don't stay in the same place—we grow.

That means we begin praying more about projects, programs, plans, and ideas than ever before. It means that we no longer merely want God to stamp the word *approval* on our plans; we want more—we want his directions in planning from the very first step. We want to be more sensitive to his leading, more aware of how God speaks in soft whispers. More in tune with his silent nudges.

That kind of commitment to seeking God's guidance will cost us, both in terms of time and independence. But it means that we will grow every day into a fuller understanding of what he wants our lives to be.

9.

Faith Gestures

"So I prayed, 'Lord, if you want me to apologize, then let the line not be busy when I call.' I waited a few minutes and dialed the number. On the second ring Alice answered," Laura said, "and I knew then that I had to apologize."

Carey had grown dissatisfied with his job. He had worked hard and he had received no pay raises and not a single hint of promotion. As we talked, he said, "I'd like you to pray with me about this situation. I've told the Lord that if I don't get a pay increase within thirty more days, I'll look somewhere else for a job." Less than two weeks later, the company offered Carey both a promotion and additional pay. He beamed when he told me about it.

Eighteen-year-old Ralph had been dating both Betty and Evelyn. One evening he got off work early and decided to visit one of them. But which one? He couldn't make up his mind. "God, when I come to the traffic signal, you guide me that way. If it's green I'll go to Betty's house. If it's red, then I'll head toward Evelyn's." The green light at the intersection determined his date that night.

A few years ago I met with a pulpit committee about becoming their pastor. They asked me and I said "I'll pray and call you within two weeks." Then I prayed, "Lord, unless you intervene and stop me, I'm going to say yes." A week later, a second pulpit committee came to hear me preach, talked to me, and also asked me to become their pastor—all within the two weeks' period. I accepted the second, believing God had intervened.

I've illustrated four times the idea of using arbitrary signs in seeking God's will. Over the years I've heard people discuss it pro and con a great deal. The real basis for this comes from the story of Gideon in the Old Testament. God spoke to him: "You're to deliver this nation from the Midianites." Possibly because of his own insecurity, or his lack of military experience, Gideon had questions. He said, "Lord, I'm putting you to the test. If you want me to do this, then I want you to show me. I'm going to lay a fleece of wool on the threshing floor. If there is dew on the fleece only and the surrounding ground is dry in the morning, then I'll know that you're with me" (see Judg. 6:36–40). That's exactly what happened: wet fleece, dry ground. The next night, needing further assurance, Gideon reversed the process. Again God fulfilled it.

At one time or another we all brush up against this matter of using arbitrary signs in seeking God's will. I suspect that the more fully we want to obey, the more carefully we consider *any* method of being more in touch with the divine will.

This "putting out the fleece" has come under criticism by many. One friend said to me, "It's like magic. You want God to do something special to make you know the right direction." He said, "I'd hate to think that I planned my whole life on whether someone answered the telephone or the light turned green." But those who want to use arbitrary signs find support elsewhere in the Bible.

Isaac's servant used this very means in selecting a wife for his master. The servant went, as Abraham instructed him, to the city of Nahor—the place from which he was to take the bride. Then he prayed for help: "Behold, I am standing by the spring of water, and daughters of the men of the city are coming out to draw water. Let the maiden to whom I shall say, 'Pray let down your jar that I may drink,' and who shall say, 'Drink, and I will water your camels'—let her be the one whom thou hast appointed for thy servant Isaac. By this I shall know that thou hast shown steadfast love to my master" (Gen. 24:13–14).

If you continue reading the account in Genesis, that's exactly what transpired. Rebekah came to the well and said the right words. Eventually she became the wife of Isaac and the mother of Jacob.

Aside from "putting out a fleece," another ancient way of discerning God's will involved the Urim and the Thummin. Even though several references appear in the Old Testament, none makes it clear how they were used. We know they were stones, kept by the high priest and used to discern the will of God. Probably he used them like this: the inquirer asked a yes or no question of God's directions. One of the two stones was designated a negative reply and the other a positive. The high priest put the Urim and the Thummin in a pouch, pulled out one and it became the answer. Kings commonly asked, "Should we go to war against the Philistines?" If the answer came back positive, victory was assured.

However, in 1 Samuel, we read that King Saul sought guidance from God, and because of his continued disobedience, "when Saul inquired of the Lord, *the Lord did not answer him*, either by dreams, or by Urim, or by prophets" (28:6). This implies more than a yes or no answer. Probably, as the use of the Urim and Thummin increased, a third stone also went into the pouch. When the priest drew that third stone it meant God declined to answer.

In the post-exilic times Ezra records, "These sought their registration among those enrolled in the genealogies, but they were not found there, and so they were excluded from the priesthood as unclean; the governor told them that they were not to partake of the most holy food, until there should be a priest to consult Urim and Thummin" (Ezra 2:62-63). Other than this brief reference and one in Nehemiah, there appears nothing more in the Old Testament about the Urim and Thummin.

The story of Jonah involves another kind of arbitrary sign. Jonah fled from God and boarded a ship heading away from Nineveh, to which God had directed him. Then a storm came up. The crew apparently sensed God had brought it upon them because of someone's sin. They said, "'Come, let us cast lots, that we may know on whose account this evil has come upon us.' So they cast lots, and the lot fell upon Jonah.'" (Jon. 1:7-8).

This casting of lots appears to have become one way to discern God's will. By a simple act of choosing a pebble or a stone, they often decided guilt or innocence.

Probably the most remarkable account of making a decision by casting lots occurs in the New Testament. After Jesus' ascension, and before the outpouring of the Holy Spirit, the remaining eleven apostles met together in an upper room, along with more than a hundred other Christians. Peter stood up and reminded them that Judas had committed suicide and, quoting from the Psalms, said they should select another to fill Judas' place.

Here's how they did it. First they prayed, "'Lord, who knowest the hearts of all men, show which one of these two thou hast chosen to take the place in this ministry and apostleship from which Judas turned aside, to go to his own place.' And they cast lots for them, and the lot fell on Matthias; and he was enrolled with the eleven apostles" (Acts 1:24–26).

It can be argued, of course, that this arbitrarily going by signs occurred prior to the coming of the Holy Spirit, which takes place in Acts 2. It can further be argued that now we have the Spirit to make decisions and they didn't.

I'm not quite so sure that's a totally valid argument. Why can't the Holy Spirit use arbitrary signs to show his will?

As I've thought about it, it seems to me that one important ingredient makes the real difference—the element of faith. When the apostles chose the successor to Judas, they believed that God would show them which of the two men he wanted. In using the Urim and Thummin, the people had complete confidence that God would declare his will.

Think again of that servant, entrusted to bring back a wife for his master's son. What a heavy pressure! But he doesn't seem to hesitate. He laid out the ground rules. "God, when I say my part and she says hers, then I'll know that's the one." He believed God would answer accordingly.

The element of faith! That makes the difference. It's saying, "God, I trust your guidance. If you let this happen, then I'll know."

Ralph's depending on the color of the traffic light to make his decision about which girl sounded a bit strange to me. *But it didn't to Ralph.* He told this to me in all seriousness. He later married Betty, too!

Maybe that says a great deal about knowing God's will. I can look at a situation and say, "The Lord has ordered it this way and now I know what to do." Another looks at the same circumstances and cries out, "God, why don't you guide me?" We all perceive life and God's purpose through different eyes and through varying amounts of faith.

Many years ago I helped another man start a church in a town where no Christian church existed. We worked for five months with minimal response. I was ready to give it up. Ray, on the other hand, said, "No, God wants a church in this town. And I'm going to stick with it, even if it takes ten years." His was the element of faith, despite the negative results. I had no such assurance, although I continued with him. Finally, people did come in, and eventually a growing congregation of Christians populated that city. It was Ray's faith that kept us working at it!

For me, that's the real answer about using arbitrary signs to discern God's will. How do *I* feel? Can I honestly accept the condition as God's communication to me? The answer to that question determines our use of arbitrary signs.

10.

Fortune Cookies, Poems, and Balloons

I keep a small piece of paper pasted on the notepad holder on my desk. It's been there nearly five years. The message it bears frequently reminds me of God's guidance.

It came about this way. When I first became the pastor of my present church, both good and bad omens met me. Some members wanted growth and change; they were eager to see the church move forward. Others appeared content with the old ways—the same number of people in every service, and everyone sitting in the same pews. I began offering my ideas, and constantly suggested new approaches. Some ideas met with immediate success; a few bombed.

After six months I had not seen the progress I had hoped for. New people had joined the church, and the number of activities had increased. But I felt the energy I was putting in did not match the results we were reaping. I hadn't run out of ideas, but I was questioning whether the ones I had would prove fruitful. I began wondering if the elders would accept more changes. "God, I don't want to disrupt what's already happening. But we have the potential for so much more. What'll I do? Do I keep pushing, trying to create a new vision? Should I draw back and allow the officers to come up with ideas?" The Lord gave no answer.

One evening the following week, Shirley and I ate in a

Chinese restaurant. At the end of the meal, the waiter brought us fortune cookies. I popped mine open, ignored the paper with the fortune on it, and ate the cookie. As I chewed on the last bit of the cookie, I picked up the printed message, prepared to laugh at the words (I'd read many of them before). Instead I read: *"Your efforts will result in much profit."*

An immediate sense of peace came to me. I knew that the Holy Spirit was communicating to me through that crumpled paper, packed months earlier in San Francisco and shipped all the way to Atlanta for me to read. It sounded crazy. I didn't even say anything to Shirley—certainly not to anyone else. After all, I didn't want people devouring fortune cookies to get guidance from the Lord. And I never experienced a second message from the Holy Spirit through a fortune cookie. But it happened once.

In the months that followed, I would think of new approaches to my work, or start dreaming of ministering more effectively. Then a caution light would flash in my mind. Frequently I would glance at the seven-word message on my notepad box, and I would have peace once again. After another year, many of the seeds I had planted bore fruit. We have had an onward-moving congregation since then. The fortune cookie message gave me the courage to keep trying.

Over the years of my spiritual pilgrimage I have come to believe that God can (and actually does!) use any method he chooses to guide his people. That's one of the exciting facets of the Christian faith—God often uses the unexpected. And we never know how he's going to speak.

During the early years of our marriage, Shirley and I found ourselves deluged with bills, which we had no adequate means of paying. I was in school, using the G.I. Bill as our main source of income. Our car needed extensive repairs. Summer was coming, and I didn't know what kind of job I could get. One day I was sitting in my mother-in-law's portion of our duplex, depressed over the situation and not knowing what to do. I looked up and noticed a framed poem on her wall. I'm sure it had been there for years, but I hadn't noticed it before. It was a poem about two birds talking. One of them asked why humans always worried and fretted. The other replied, "Maybe they don't have a heavenly Father to watch over them as we do."

I read the poem several times, each time realizing that the Lord was using that message to calm my spirits. That very afternoon I found a summer job, and the mechanic who repaired my car allowed me three months to pay for it—with no extra charges.

Here's another type of unusual guidance. A friend stood in line at the airport, waiting to buy a ticket. She was going to a distant city for a job interview. She had doubts—of her own qualifications, of her ability to fit into the job—she even wondered if she'd like the working conditions. Was God really leading her to make the move? She thought of the money she was spending, and the fact that, if she didn't get the position, it would be wasted. All these thoughts kept flashing through her mind as she stood in line. Just before she reached the counter, an elderly woman, who had been buying a ticket, started to walk away from it. She stopped by my friend and said, "Dear, God loves you, and he's taking care of you." Then she hurried on, saying nothing to anyone else.

My friend said, "I felt as though heaven had opened up to me and God had created that old lady with a message just for me." My friend had the interview, took the job, and has stayed with that company several years.

Far-out guidance? You bet!

What about Jonah and the whale? Quite a strange way for God to communicate. And in the last chapter of the same book, the Lord spoke to Jonah using a dried-up vine! Believers of old often had strange dreams. They cast lots. And they always recognized God in action.

Some instances of guidance described in the Bible seem just as far-fetched as guidance from a fortune cookie! One day, for instance, a young man named Saul, along with his servant, searched for donkeys that had gone astray. Someone suggested that they consult a prophet named Samuel. They did, and the old man said, "They have been found" (1 Sam. 9:20). The prophet then said that God had chosen Saul as the first king of Israel.

As the prophet talked, it appeared that God had actually sent the animals astray so that Saul would search for them and meet up with the prophet. A rather strange way for a guiding God to act!

Gideon had a freakish kind of word from the Lord. Even after his incident with the fleece (see Judg. 6:36–40), he still needed assurance from the Lord. God spoke and said that, if he still needed further encouragement, he and Purah, a servant, should go to the outposts of the enemy camps and listen to what the enemies said. They went, and as they arrived there, they heard a man telling a dream to his comrade: "'Behold, I dreamed a dream; and lo, a cake of barley bread tumbled into the camp of Midian, and it came to the tent, and struck it so that it fell, and turned it upside down, so that the tent lay flat.' And his comrade answered, 'This is no other than the sword of Gideon the son of Joash, a man of Israel; into his hand God has given Midian and all the host'" (Judg. 7:13–14).

Throughout the Bible people received guidance from dreams, such as the one in which an angel appeared to Joseph, telling him that he should take Mary as his wife (see Matt. 1:10). The wise men received their guidance, apparently, by following a star.

We've trapped ourselves in a rational world. Everything must have a ring of logic and be scientifically verified or we don't believe it. We're gullible about accepting statistics, research, and experiments. But if we limit ourselves only to what is verifiable, we shut ourselves off from many of God's exciting communications.

Here's one way that I've found helpful for looking at God's leading. Back in my student days, the professors and text writers stressed a characteristic of God they called his *transcendence*. They used this three-syllable word to say that God is both within this world and beyond it. On the other hand, we humans are in this world, because we're part of his creation. We have no choice. Because of his love, God chooses to be part of our world.

In much the same way, a counselor is not part of his patient's situation. The patient's problems are not his problems. But as he listens they become his as well, because of concern. The same applies to a parent. A mother hears that her daughter failed a history test. It's not the mother's problem, but her love for her own makes her part of the situation. "We'll work together on your lessons every night," she might say, or "That means no evening television until your grades improve."

God is absolutely free, owing nothing to his creation. He involves himself in our lives, not out of any necessity, but out of his love for us.

This means that although God is, by his own choice, always present, he must also break through the limitations of our understanding in order to communicate with us. He chooses to break into our well-ordered world, and he does it in hundreds of ways.

One way God breaks through to us is the Bible. We Christians believe it's a special kind of book, but not because of its antiquity. We affirm that this book comes from God, and that the writers were moved upon in some supernatural way to write the texts. God uses the Bible in directing us. But sometimes the Holy Spirit steps outside the pages in his moment-to-moment guidance. The Spirit doesn't contradict himself, but he doesn't limit himself, either.

I want to be open for God to speak in any manner he chooses—and at any time. I don't read tea leaves, own a ouija board, or read horoscope projections in the newspapers. I have never had my palm read or been to a séance. But I attempt to remain open for God to break into my sheltered world, surprising me with his choice of communication.

One day I walked through a large shopping mall. I had spent more money than I had expected, consumed more time than I had allotted, and was already late for an appointment. People blocked my path as I tried to hurry. I began to feel my body tensing and my mind clicking off the additional minutes that I'd be late.

Just then I glanced up and saw a young boy, sitting on his father's shoulders, holding a balloon—a balloon with a smiling face. Just noticing that balloon seemed to change my whole attitude. I smiled at the small boy, slowed down my pace, and continued moving through the mall—but this time no rushing, no frenzied pace. As I walked I was saying, "Thanks Lord, thanks for reminding me to smile, to be aware that you're with me and everything's OK in the world."

Does it matter *how* the Spirit leads? It matters only that he does lead!

11.

The Devil Wouldn't Let Me Go!

"That old devil!" the evangelist thundered. "He's trying to work in me and in you! We try to do God's will and the devil keeps hanging onto our coattails." He threw his coat angrily on the floor.

"I'm free—for awhile—and then that old red-eyed devil comes back again. Tempting me. Fighting me. The devil just won't let me go!"

I couldn't have been more than ten when I attended that tent revival. The preacher frightened me. For weeks afterwards, I didn't like to be alone in the dark. Walking down the street, I'd keep turning around, afraid the devil had sneaked up behind and was ready to pounce.

Eventually I outgrew the fear of the stalking creature. I assumed that the rest of the world had, too. But not long ago I realized that this kind of thinking still troubles many.

For instance, I sat in a church service where people had the opportunity to give testimonies. One middle-aged lady stood up, told of her many troubles, and said, "The devil just won't let me alone. He chases me everywhere I go." For the next few minutes she gave us a run-down of all the methods the devil used to hinder her spiritual growth.

A friend, with whom I had visited the church, leaned over and whispered, "She seems to know more about the devil than she does about Jesus."

It made me wonder if that's not the way with some other

people. They're more involved with talking about Satan's activities than with talking about God's; they're filled more with fear of the Evil One than with love for the Holy One.

I see several obvious dangers in overstressing the devil's involvement.

1. *We get our minds off God.* It's a way of saying we get taken up with the negative and don't recognize the positive. We're always looking back over our spiritual shoulders, checking to see if the devil is working. We don't move ahead because we're always controlled by the past.

2. *We blame the devil for our own failings.* In Africa, a young orphan worked for us on the mission to earn the required school fees for junior high school. He worked well for almost a year. Then we noticed things missing—articles of clothing, small amounts of meat, a few vegetables. Finally I actually caught him stealing.

"The devil got into me, sir," the young man cried out. "I did not intend to steal from you, but the evil one took over and caused me to do such things."

He was hiding behind a cultural barrier. Among his particular tribe, and especially among non-Christians, one never admitted wrongdoing. One could blame an evil spirit, an outside source, even another person. As missionaries taught them about a forgiving God, they always taught them to say, "I have sinned."

The young man, who had once made a profession of faith, suddenly switched back to the language of his culture. He tried to convince me that the boy was innocent and that only the devil should be blamed.

The devil works enough as it is. We don't need to offer him any unearned honor.

3. *We not only blame the devil for our failures, but we also fail to face responsibility for our actions.*

If we can blame an outside force, then we have nothing to confess—nothing to repent of or to change.

Once when we were still young children, my mother brought bananas home from the store. As usual, she bought them a little on the green side and put them in a dark drawer until they ripened. I told my two brothers about the bananas. The next day

Mel, two years younger and ten years bolder, decided he wanted one of those bananas. He sneaked into the kitchen, found the bananas, took one, and almost made it to the back door when Mom walked in. She saw the fruit in his hand.

The spanking started. "Cec made me do it! Cec made me do it!" he yelled between cries of pain.

"Did not!" I yelled in self-defense.

"I don't care who put you up to it," Mom said as she continued to spank Mel, "*You* took the banana."

That's a view of how I see us spiritually. The devil works behind the scenes and tempts us, but we have to bear the responsibility for our own actions. Adam, after his failure in the garden, tried to blame the woman. She, in turn, blamed the serpent. But God punished Adam and held him responsible for what he had done.

The same applies to us. When we obey any outside voice, we still have to shoulder our responsibility.

That's one group of people—the ones who put too much emphasis on the devil. When they want God's leadership, they're always stopping to check out the devil's activities, then make their decision before the enemy hears. They refer often to satanic hindrances and quote from an incident in the book of Daniel (see Dan. 10:12–13), in which God heard the prophet the first time he prayed but was hindered from answering by the Prince of the Kingdom of Persia (a Satanic name).

This group expends much energy on outsmarting the devil. But if they take the work of Satan too seriously, most of us don't take him seriously enough. Many otherwise conservative folks avoid talking about the great Deceiver.

We even feel uncomfortable with terms such as "demon possession" or "exorcism." That kind of language doesn't fit the modern mind. We prefer the sophisticated phrases such as "manic depressive" or "schizoid personality." Yet even using psychological terms doesn't really settle the problem.

I'm not trying to equate mental illness with demon possession. The ancients had an entirely different way of looking at life. They attributed everything evil as coming from Satan.

Even so, we still have to wrestle with incidents in the Bible where Jesus called evil spirits to come out of people. They all received immediate healing. To smooth it over by saying, "He was only speaking in first-century language" doesn't play fair with the New Testament. When the biblical accounts record that the demonic spirits spoke, can we shrug it off by saying, "That's the way primitive people understood it"? It's hardly being faithful to the biblical accounts.

How can we grasp the book of Job without understanding the evil powers? Even if the scenes in heaven where Satan and God speak are metaphorical, the lesson we easily see is this: we serve a holy Spirit. An unholy spirit also works in the universe.

This doesn't suggest we spend our time placating Satan. But it does mean, as in the words of the apostle Paul, "We are not contending against flesh and blood" (Eph. 6:12). We fight spiritual battles against spiritual forces. When we seek God's guidance, we'll often have spiritual forces working against us.

Here are several conclusions I've reached about the work of the devil and God's guidance.

First, we don't need to constantly search for the devil. He's at work "going to and fro upon the earth" (Job 1:7). We don't need to fill our minds with his tactics.

We need to recognize that we fight spiritual battles. But we don't fight them by constantly rebuking the devil. We fight in the name of the Lord.

In *Pilgrim's Progress*, the hero, Christian, travels toward the celestial city. One day he sees a lion on the path in front of him. He remembers the verse (1 Pet. 5:8) that "the devil prowls around like a roaring lion, seeking some one to devour," and the poor man quakes with fear. Then he hears a voice saying, "Don't be afraid." As the pilgrim nears, he sees something: the lion is still there, but he's chained, and the chain won't allow the animal to reach the path. As long as Pilgrim walks in the very middle of the road, he's safe. That's still our message today!

Finally, we can trust God to provide victory for us. Remember Job again. God never told him of the devil's involvement, so far as we know. He lived in hope of God's intervention and maintained a high faith in God. And God carried the man through to ultimate victory.

And while we need to be aware of the lures of the devil, victory comes through keeping our eyes on Jesus Christ.

While we don't want to ignore Satan's influences or hindrances, our faith in Jesus Christ enables us to overcome all his snares. God will guide us. He's still got the lion chained.

12.

Declaring God's Will

"Why do you keep struggling?" Ken asked out of deep concern.

"Because," I replied, "I want to follow the Lord's will. I can't seem to get an answer. I'm praying until I know."

"Why don't you simply declare God's will and then go on?" he answered.

Ken explained a method he had used for more than twenty years when he encountered perplexing situations. "When I come to those moments of decision and can't seem to get a clear view, I arbitrarily declare God's will."

Ken envisions a traveler walking down a straight road. Eventually he comes to a place where the road forks to the left and to the right. Which way should he go?

"I pray about it. I want God's will and he knows it. If nothing comes to me as a word from the Lord, I make my decision by saying, 'This road is the one.' I declare one of them as God's will."

"But what if it isn't the right decision?" I asked.

"Before long I begin to get signs like 'detour' or 'bridge out,' or he uses some other way to let me know I've taken the wrong fork." Ken also mentioned Acts 16:1–10, in which the Apostle Paul attempted to visit Bithynia and God halted him. Then he moved on to Troas. That night God spoke to his servant in a dream, directing him to go into Europe.

Ken said, "We have no way of knowing how God stopped Paul. I've always suspected that it might have been as simple as not having a boat available to travel. Or not having enough money for the trip. Maybe one of his helpers got sick the night before they left. I've even thought Paul may not have had a sense of peace and that was enough to tell him."

Ken told me that he had enough confidence in God's desire to lead to believe that God will stop his people from going too far in the wrong direction. He compared this to how he prays for the sick. "When someone is sick, I pray for healing by the Divine Physician. I ask for a total recovery. I pray with a positive attitude. And I've witnessed several remarkable responses to prayer. On the other hand, they don't all get better. But whether they get better or not, I pray for God to deliver them and expect to see it happen. Then it's up to him. And I feel the same way about guidance. I assume that God guides. He'll stop me if I'm wrong."

"You make it sound so easy," I replied.

"I don't know about being easy," he said, "but it's practical. I pray for guidance. But, frankly, not many things make me stay on my knees for long periods of time or keep nagging at me for days or even weeks. It has to involve a very crucial decision to get me that tangled up."

Ken mentioned that when it came to matters such as a job change, moving, buying a car—the big decisions—he made quite sure he sensed God's will before taking a step. "But we don't have that many major decisions every day. I'm talking about the everyday kind of things, like asking God how to use my time, or whether I should participate in a new program at the church or join a health spa. Those kinds of decisions I like to make quickly. If I don't, I struggle over them, allow them to sap my energy. I get little else done, wondering what God wants. When I declare God's will, I don't think about it again."

I liked Ken's response, remembering times I had agonized over decisions. Sometimes I could have settled them easily by using Ken's method. My friend added, "When we honestly put God first, his will isn't hard to find. I pray to give God a chance to speak through the Bible or circumstances or in some other way. When no word comes, and all options seem about the same, I declare one of them as God's direction. I then move accordingly."

While Ken was chairman of the Spiritual Life Committee of a church, he wrote a gifted teacher-preacher and asked him to come for a series of meetings. "We'd like you to teach on the will of God," Ken wrote.

He waited two weeks and no reply. He wrote a second letter. He waited two more weeks. Finally Ken phoned and asked, "Brother, did you get my letters?"

"Oh, yes, I received both of them."

"You never answered either of them."

"I've been praying for the Lord to guide me. I didn't want to write until I heard from him."

My friend said, "In that case, don't come. If it takes you that long to know his will, I'm not sure you can help us. So I'm withdrawing the request. I'm going to help by giving you peace. I'm declaring to you that it's not God's will for you to come."

"See how simple it is?" Ken chuckled. He then contacted a second person, who accepted within a few days, and the special meetings went well.

Ken gets impatient with people who spend too much time trying to know the right direction. "Those people give the impression God doesn't want to speak. It's as though they have to coax the Lord into sending them a message. They also act as if every situation in life becomes a life or death issue."

My friend Velma agrees with Ken. She shared her experience of working in a church-related preschool program in which five workers took care of thirty-four children. "Whenever a crisis erupted (which happened regularly)," Velma said, "it got to be a real problem. I was the outsider in that church group. They all ran into their chapel and sought divine wisdom. That's okay, of course. And they really prayed—sometimes for a full hour. *But* they left me with all thirty-four children. I was so busy trying to handle all those little ones—their crying, fussing, and demanding attention—I didn't have time to think about the Lord's will."

Velma concluded by saying, "I could have told them the Holy Spirit's answer. He was saying, 'Watch the children. That's your first duty. Worry about other things later.'"

For me, declaring God's will and acting upon it has been helpful since Ken shared it. As I've thought about it, that attitude suggests three significant things.

1. It's a step of faith. When you look at two or more choices in front of you and can't seem to know which way to go, you make your choice. You say, "God, I declare this as your will."

Doing this puts our faith on the line. It means we trust God's intervention if we've made the wrong decision.

I liken declaring God's will to Paul's statement that we have the mind of Christ (1 Cor. 2:16). When I want God to lead, I submit myself to his leadership. If I don't receive a distinct impression or guidance, then I step out on faith. In the absence of a directive word, I make my choice, believing I have the mind of Christ.

2. It's a mark of maturity. "Most decisions in life aren't irreversible," Ken said. "Sometimes we make mistakes when we want to know God's will. If we go down the wrong path, all we have to do is reverse our direction."

Doing that requires openness. We look at our mistakes, acknowledge them, and say, "OK, I goofed. Now I leave that behind." That's spiritual maturity in action!

But I've learned that reversing myself isn't always easy.

Years ago I involved myself in a certain situation. I had prayed, been sure of the Spirit's leading, and told several people. One of them, not a particularly close friend, responded cynically. "Yeah? We'll see," he said.

Later I had to reverse my direction. The cynic asked me what happened. At first I thought of justifying my action (we can always find ways to clear ourselves). Instead I said, "I guess I made a mistake. I really thought I was doing the right thing, but now I see it differently."

I waited, expecting sneering words of advice. Instead he smiled. "You know, I'm glad you said that. You've always seemed so cocksure about everything. Your floundering shows me how human you are."

I matured through the experience. After all, there's no shame in going back. The real fool is one who keeps going simply because he declared that was the right direction.

3. It reflects a committed relationship. This is the most significant implication. When I look at my options and pick one, I'm saying, "Father, I'm your child. This course of action appears good, but you know the end from the beginning. You have greater wisdom. Change my direction if I'm wrong."

The commitment works in both directions. My praying and seeking guidance tells God where I am. My faith tells me where God is. We're both committed to each other in all of life's decisions.

As I continue growing in the Christian life, I believe the mind of Christ is *in me*. That concept gives me a sense of peace when I declare God's will.

The first time I ever tried Ken's suggestion was when a situation arose demanding a decision within one hour. It involved making three phone calls—and one party was leaving town. Nothing came as I prayed.

"Okay, Lord, then I declare as the will of God . . ." and made my choice.

But, unlike Ken, I had second thoughts. What if I chose wrongly? What if an underlying desire had influenced my decision? Like a low-lying cloud which wants to burst with rain, the incident hung over me all day.

The next morning, in my devotional reading, I read these two verses:

The steps of good men are directed by the Lord. He delights in each step they take. If they fall it isn't fatal, for the Lord holds them with his hand (Ps. 37:23,24,TLB).

"Thanks, Lord, that's good enough for me."

13.

Disobedient Guidance

It's not easy to admit that at times I've disobeyed God's directions, but I have. I can't recall specific instances of deliberate defiance, in which I've said, "God, I don't care what you want; this is what I'm going to do."

My disobedience has most often come through convincing myself that God really wanted me to move in a particular direction. Many Christians have experienced this. We've wanted something so badly, prayed so fervently, and claimed every biblical promise we could think of. Eventually, we convinced ourselves of God's will. "Lord," we prayed, "if this isn't your will, speak to me." We may then have acted very much like the child stuffing fingers in both ears and saying, "I can't hear you."

Or perhaps we disobeyed in entirely different ways. Remember the story of David and Bathsheba? She was another man's wife. David already had several wives and concubines. But he saw the woman and lusted after her.

One day as I read the story of David and Bathsheba, I paused and reflected. This man—this very special person—how could he do such a thing? If King Saul had done it, who would have been surprised? But David?

He's the one who wrote all those beautiful shepherd psalms, the one who sang and danced and played his instrument for the Lord. We find descriptions of him as a man after God's own heart. To think of David succumbing to such sin staggers the mind. Surely not a man who knew God so intimately!

Wasn't he the same man who, although chased by King Saul, refused to hurt his oppressor? Although several opportunities to kill the king in the night occurred, David always held back. He had such reverence for the injunction by the prophet, "Touch not the Lord's anointed," that he would not allow himself or his men to harm Saul. He reasoned that God had anointed Saul as king, and as long as God kept the man on the throne David would not interfere. He even ordered the execution of a man who participated in the actual killing of Saul!

And yet we read of this man committing adultery, then using the sin of murder to cover up!

I've come to the conclusion that David didn't intend to disobey God—he simply did it without giving God a chance to talk to him.

Another story occurs in the Old Testament. A fellow named Achan stole gold, silver, and expensive garments when the Israelites destroyed Jericho. Ordinarily, victors divided the spoils of battle, but in this particular instance, God had said, "Take nothing."

Later, when caught, Achan confessed, "When I saw among the spoil a beautiful mantle from Shinar, and two hundred shekels of silver, and a bar of gold weighing fifty shekels, then I coveted them, and took them . . ." (Josh. 7:21).

Achan didn't pause to pray, to think, to consider the consequences. He acted on impulse. Perhaps David did the same with Bathsheba.

In reflection, I can think of times when I've disobeyed God's will simply because I didn't ask for his guidance. I didn't pray, "Lord, is this pleasing to you?" I merely acted, and the result was disobedience.

I don't like to fail God. I don't want anyone else to fail. But we all do; all of us disobey him at one time or the other. Then what?

I'd like to put as much emphasis as possible upon saying, "Don't." At the same time, however, God is always saying, "But if you do . . ."

That's the purpose of Jesus' death on Calvary—not merely to forgive our past, but to cleanse us on a daily basis as well. I once talked to a devout young Christian who was depressed because he had failed God by losing his temper in an argument. He finally said, "I know Jesus Christ forgave everything in my life before I knew him. But now I'm on my own. Now I have to keep myself clean."

In our heads we know the young man was wrong in saying that. Unfortunately, many of us live in that same vein. We forget that Jesus Christ is the *continuous* sacrifice for sins, always the forgiving one!

And when we do sin—by ignorance or by rationalizing, or even deliberately—God still forgives and leads us to the right path again.

As a matter of fact, going through periods of disobedience may be one of the most effective ways we learn how God leads us. Even our spiritual blackouts can become teaching instruments.

1. *For one thing, we learn caution.* I often think of the purported Chinese proverb, "Once bitten, twice careful." We know how to look for danger. We're less susceptible the second time.

I see this principle in my jogging. In one area where I run alongside the main road, people have broken an almost straight path on the edge of the field. I've run on that section often enough to know its smoothness is deceptive. In a few places the grass covers holes or sharp stones. One morning I twisted my ankle because I wasn't careful and didn't watch the ground. I'll never be careless in that section again.

2. *We learn to fortify ourselves.* All of us have weak spots in our personalities. Awareness of our weaknesses enables us to prepare in advance when we know we're going to face those situations.

I have a formerly fat friend who realizes this acutely. Whenever he goes out to eat, he asks his wife to be a reminder of his consumption level. He makes it a point to drink several glasses of water or tea at the early part of the meal. He eats slowly, never takes more than three bites without pausing for a sip of water. He also prays a great deal for God to enable him to overcome the temptation to give in to his appetite.

3. *We learn by suffering.* During my early days as a Christian, a group of us sat at a table drinking cokes. Someone asked what I

thought of Alice, and my answer, while honest, showed no tact or kindness. A few days later, I saw Alice at church. She gave me a cold nod, and started to walk away. Then she came back and said, "I heard what you said about me. Think anything you like. But don't come around with a big smile and act like a friend."

What had been passed on to her? I don't know. It may have been exaggerated, but it hurt Alice. And I suffered because I had hurt someone deeply. Even though I apologized to her, the damage was done. How much better it would have been if, when asked my opinion of Alice, I had silently prayed for the Lord to guide my words and allow me to speak, as the Apostle Paul says, "the truth in love?" or perhaps even to remain silent.

Sometimes, in order to grow, we have to experience the effects of disobedience. We have to know what it's like *not* to be led by God's Spirit.

Psalm 51 presents a vivid picture of suffering. That plaintive chapter tells the anguish of David's heart. It's the cry of a man who has lost the sense of divine direction and wants to find it again. But if we read the books of 1 and 2 Samuel, we see that God again led David after the incident with Bathsheba. He apparently learned from his disobedience and suffering.

In 2 Chronicles 18 and 19, we read the story of another man who learned the hard way. Judah's king, Jehoshaphat, made an alliance with Ahab, king of Israel. They decided to fight together at Ramoth-gilead, although the prophet Micaiah warned against the venture: "If you return in peace, the Lord has not spoken by me" (2 Chron. 18:27).

In the battle, an archer mortally wounded Ahab. Jehoshaphat fled from the battlefield and "returned in safety to his house in Jerusalem. But Jehu the son of Hanani the seer went out to meet him, and said to King Jehoshaphat, 'Should you help the wicked and love those who hate the Lord? Because of this, wrath has gone out against you from the Lord. Nevertheless some good is found in you, for you destroyed the Asherahs [i.e., idols] out of the land, and have set your heart to seek God'" (2 Chron. 19:1–3).

After that experience, Jehoshaphat became a ruler who put God first and exhorted his people to do the same.

4. We also learn the consequences of not being led by the Holy

Spirit. It's easy to get cocky, especially after the Lord has done a significant thing for us. It happened to godly Joshua.

The victories had come easily because the Lord was leading the new nation into the promised land. The Israelites' fame spread; people feared their power and acknowledged that the Living God fought with them.

Then a wily group of people from Gibeon had an idea. They came to Joshua and his people and deceived them into thinking they had come from a far country. They pleaded, "Make a covenant with us." Joshua and the leaders did; they wrote a treaty and spared their lives. Only later did they discover their mistake. The writer of Joshua records that they "did not ask direction from the Lord" (Josh. 9:14).

That mistake proved costly. The Gibeonites became water carriers and woodcutters for the congregation. But, in later years, they also proved a source of trouble within the nation. That trouble could easily have been avoided—if the leaders had simply asked God's directions!

Some of us, and in particular instances, learn about guidance through disobedience. We learn after the fact. By knowing what we did wrong and experiencing the ensuing misery, we become more determined than ever to get on the right path.

A friend named Bob told me that he never really came to grips with life, never reached a place of deep commitment, until he finally turned to God for directions. For years Bob had been a Christian—at least he had considered himself one. But he wanted to be a success in his business. He prayed every day, "God, make me a good businessman. Help me make money so that I can . . ." and he listed all the things he could do for God, all the while thinking of what the money could do for him.

Bob reached a point of high success in his business. But it was also a time of emptiness, and he finally said, "Lord, is this all there is in life?" The Lord's leading took him in a completely different direction. He left his position as top salesman for a plastic products company, and started over again as a personnel manager of a different firm. Although he doesn't have the annual income he did a dozen years ago, Bob has a happiness he never believed possible.

We can learn from the negative as well as from the positive. It's always easier on us when we get guidance from the Lord, obey, and go from there. But sometimes . . . sometimes we have to learn by disobeying first.

I recall that, as a very young boy, I watched my mother baking one morning. She added vanilla extract to a mixture, and one whiff of the flavoring made me want to drink the whole bottle. My mother said, "It's not good to drink. It's only good when it's baked into something."

A few minutes later, she left the kitchen. Almost immediately, I had the vanilla bottle in my hands; I unscrewed the lid and took a healthy swallow. Then I gagged and screamed and spit, but nothing seemed to take the bitter taste out of my mouth. My mother rushed back into the kitchen, saw what I had done, and laughed heartily. "Well, I guess that's one lesson you've learned."

But such a hard way to learn.

Isn't it better to learn by obeying?

14.

Going Home Again

"I can never be as close to the Lord as I once was," Ella said softly, as she twisted her handkerchief. "Not ever."

"Why not?" I asked.

"Because—because I had a chance once, and I turned my back on God. Deliberately, too. I knew I was doing wrong, and at the time it didn't seem to matter to me what God thought. Now I'm trying to find God in my life once again. I want to take what little God will give me, because I know I can't ever be as close as I was before."

I've heard others voice the same feelings. When I try to pin them down, they usually talk in vague terms about losing their first love, about deliberately forsaking the directive will of God, about going too far down the path.

I don't know how Ella and others arrived at that kind of theology, and I don't believe it! Actually, I think it's a demonic ploy to keep God's people from seeking the best available to them.

His will is always the best. We might miss it on the first go-around—even a second time. But God keeps extending his hand. He continually wants us to hop on board. And he wants us to go first class, not steerage!

Somehow the idea that we can't go home again permeates our thinking. Aside from that being the title of a popular novel of a bygone generation, that statement is quoted frequently, almost as though it deserves recognition as the eleventh commandment. If we mean that we can't recapture that which is lost, that's true. We can't relive anything.

In F. Scott Fitzgerald's short story, "Babylon Revisited," the main character visits his hometown again after many years. He has dreamed of what it used to be; now he's come home. And it's not the same anymore.

I can understand. I remember visiting my hometown again after I had been in the military service for less than a year. Nothing was the same—especially my old friends. They had filled their lives with new people and other activities. I became the intruder. From that time on, whenever I visited my hometown, it was always as a stranger. And I, too, began to parrot the words, "You can't go home again."

I remember talking to Donna just before we went to Kenya. She had grown up there, but had not returned since her high school days. A decade later, she advised us on everything from the economy to tribal customs to what goods we could not buy.

But when we reached Africa, we realized that Donna had described a country twelve years in the past. She was looking back at a country and a people which no longer existed.

In a sense, it's true that we can't go back home again. We can't go back to innocence and naïveté. We can't go back to a period of time that no longer exists.

But there's also a side of untruth to the statement. If we mean that God closes the door on us, I don't believe it.

One twenty-five-year-old man sat in my office, clenching his teeth, trying not to get emotional. He almost cried as he told me how he had failed God in his younger years. "I've always wanted to serve him, to be a preacher. But now it's too late."

"Why?" I asked.

"What do you mean, 'Why?'"

"Why do you say it's too late?"

"Because I failed God. I did a lot of things I shouldn't have done." He then listed half a dozen failures in his life.

"But don't you believe that God forgives?"

"Sure, he forgives, but—"

"No, that's not right. God doesn't forgive with strings attached. He doesn't add words like *but*. He forgives, *Period*."

81

The young man didn't go into the ministry, but he did become a dynamic worker in a local congregation. He suddenly realized that everything wasn't lost. He accepted the fact that God's forgiveness covers all our sins, that we *can* go home again; we can start over.

Interestingly, I once shared this experience with a devout Christian couple. Upon hearing it, the wife said immediately, "Yes, I believe God forgives, but—"

And I stopped her, too.

"Don't add another word. When God forgives, he forgives, doesn't he?" I may have been a bit too sharp, but I saw that we're constantly adding on to things, always trying to tell people how to live, always sure we understand the will of God better than someone else.

"But—but he's been married and divorced!" she stammered.

"And you think, then, that he can never fully enjoy God's guidance in his life—God's guiding will?"

"I don't see how. He had his chances and turned aside. I don't think God dooms him to hell, but—"

"What about David the King?" I asked, as the story of David and Bathsheba popped into my head. "The King of Israel—the great leader—already had several wives. Then he committed adultery with Bathsheba, and had her husband killed to cover up Bathsheba's pregnancy. Do you think David walked as close to God afterwards?"

"Well, uh—"

I thought of other great heroes of faith. Peter denied Jesus, but he still became "the rock." Abraham had a few failures in his path, but became the father of a great nation.

Then I remembered the story of Jonah.

Jonah knew God's will: go to Ninevah and preach against the sins of the people. He ran from God, ended up in the sea and inside the great fish. Then Jonah had a spiritual renewal, and the fish vomited him onto the shore.

What happened next? "Then the word of the Lord came to Jonah the second time, saying, 'Arise, go to Nineveh, that great city, and proclaim to it the message that I tell you'" (Jon. 3:1,2).

The most exciting fact in the book comes in those verses: "The word of the Lord came to Jonah *the second time*" (italics mine).

82

Jonah did go to Nineveh, and proclaimed the Word of God. He had another chance. God still wanted to lead the prophet.

In a sense, Jonah went home again.

If the story of the prodigal son teaches us anything about forgiveness, it teaches us not only that the penitent son went home again, but that the loving father waited with arms wide open. He said, "This is my son."

When we return home, life won't be the same as before. We're different. More experienced. Hopefully, wiser. It may also be that we're more compassionate! Maybe we're a bit more understanding about other people who fail.

Years ago, a young lady I knew graduated from high school and headed off to college. One of the elders in the church said, half-jokingly, "I hope she gets drunk once while she's in school."

His attitude shocked me. Anne was one of the leaders of our youth department. She was an example to the rest. I told him so.

"She's also a self-righteous little snit," he said softly. "She needs to fall flat on her face a couple of times so she can be a little more sensitive to the others who've already fallen."

The elder may have said it crudely, but I understood his meaning. There are those who have to experience failure before they can become compassionate people.

For others, making major failures hurts to the point of absolute discouragement. To them, it's like having to settle for second place in the spiritual realm. But don't believe that—not for a single instant!

We all have regrets. We all make mistakes. All of us (if we're honest) can think in terms of "If only I had . . ."

Yet one thing I'm convinced of as a Christian is that the Lord is always picking us up, always saying, "Ready to start again? Ready for a new try?"

I remember when I taught my three children to swim. Wanda, older and more nervous, and also a little more aware of the dangers of drowning, had the most difficult time. She'd start to sink, she'd scream out, her head would go under the water, and she'd panic. One time she declared, "I'm never going to learn to swim. I can't do it."

I kept assuring her she could. And eventually she made it! She sputtered and gagged and cried a few times, but eventually Wanda became an excellent swimmer.

I often think of God as the kind of parent figure who is always saying, "Try it again. We can make it this time." Or another way of putting it, "The word of the Lord came to Cec (or Mary or Paul or Robert or Evelyn) a second time, saying 'Go . . .'"

When we get the word the second time, our abilities may not be the same. But God still wants to guide us. I think of an old friend of mine, Art—raised in the church, the son of a minister, his older brother a soon-to-be ordained pastor, his sister married to a minister. Art looked like the black sheep. He kept resisting any pull from the Lord.

But one night he almost lost his life in a car accident. He lived—with 50 percent of his hearing gone and a deep scar on his cheek. He later told me that during those moments of hovering between life and death, a song kept going through his mind. It was an old gospel hymn he had sung many times in his father's services: "I'll Go Where You Want Me to Go."

In his weakened condition he said, "Lord, whatever is left of me is yours. You may not have much to work with, but you're going to get all that I am."

Art died recently—after another thirty-eight years of faithful service to the Lord. Today many Africans give thanks to God for Art's life, because through him they came in contact with the gospel.

And all that happened because Art listened, and said, "yes," to the God who comes to us the second time.

15.

When God Hides

The other day I skimmed through an article called "You Can
Know God's Will." In it the author asserted that we can always
receive guidance from the Lord. He concluded with seven
simple steps for discovering the mind of God. While he didn't
call them infallible, he hinted as much.

Years ago I read a tract by George Mueller, that great man of
faith from Bristol, England. It was entitled "How I Discern the
Will of God." In it, he also gave several steps.

Nearly every time I pick up a piece of literature on the will of
God, the author offers me positive teachings on how to discover
what God wants for me. We need positive material in that area.
But what happens when we honestly don't know God's will?
After we've followed all the prescribed steps?

I asked that question of several friends as we ate lunch
together. They all had an answer for me. One replied immediately, "Nonsense! We always know. And if we don't, we
simply wait. God always comes to those who wait."

A second blurted out, "Then sin is blocking God from
speaking. You probably need to recognize whatever stands
between you and God, confess it, and put it away." She even
sang a chorus of the old hymn, "Nothing Between."

Another added, "'If I regard iniquity in my heart, the Lord
will not hear me.' And Peter says that the Lord closes his ears to
the wicked, but opens them to the righteous."

Someone else suggested that I persevere. "Keep pounding on

the portals of heaven until he showers his answer upon you."

Still the answers came: "Maybe you're asking the wrong question. Maybe you need to obey what you already know instead of asking for new directions."

"Are you living in total submission to Jesus Christ?" one man asked as he leaned across the table. "Not just the absence of sin, but an unreserved yielding to God. When I don't know God's will, then I know I need to make a fuller dedication of my life to Jesus."

A quiet voice asked, "Have you searched your motives? Are they pure before God? Do you want to know in order to obey more perfectly? God won't show you unless you intend to obey."

My head began spinning. Not that they were actually wrong—not any of them. Each of the answers I heard has validity. What disturbed me was how quick my friends were to give simplistic answers to a complex question. They even had side discussions among themselves.

God wants his people to obey. And to obey they need his directions. His written Word, helpful as it is (and I never want to minimize that), isn't enough! The Bible never makes provision for every situation. We need the Holy Spirit speaking to give us specific directions in specific instances.

I appreciate my friends' wanting to rescue God's honor. Yet none of them seriously considered the possibility that God might choose *not* to make his will known. They had to pile answers on me quickly to avoid entertaining that thought.

As they spoke, interrupting each other and reexplaining, I recalled a time when my dad handed me his set of keys. He wanted something out of the trunk of his car. But Dad owned two cars and a truck! I counted twelve keys on the small chain. By immediately eliminating those that obviously weren't for a vehicle, I brought the number down to six. I tried each until I found the one that fit the trunk.

Is that one way we discover God's will—we try one method, and then another, and still another, until we stumble onto the answer? In some cases we might have to do just that!

Most of us have prayed and received immediate answers (as I've expressed in other chapters). But sometimes . . . sometimes no answer appears. No matter how many keys we try in the lock, it doesn't open. There have been times in my own life when I have tried every conceivable method and nothing happened. At times like that I think of "The God Who Hides Himself." That's one of the names Isaiah called him:

> Truly, thou art a God who hidest thyself, O God of Israel, the Savior (Isa. 45:15).

> For a brief moment I forsook you, but with great compassion I will gather you. In overflowing wrath for a moment I hid my face from you, but with everlasting love I will have compassion on you, says the Lord, your Redeemer (Isaiah 54:7–8).

The context implies that God hides himself because of the nation's sin. But I think there are other times when God hides himself.

Remember King Hezekiah (see 2 Kings 20:1–21)? Envoys from Babylon visited the kingdom of Judea, and Hezekiah foolishly showed them all his treasures. The writer of Chronicles records that God stepped out of the picture and "let Hezekiah go his own way only in order to test his character" (2 Chron. 32:31, TEV).

God wanted to know what was in the king's heart—and he remained silent.

Job presents the classic case in the Bible. The devil used every weapon against Job, and the suffering man didn't understand. The reader knows that God allowed Satan to kill Job's family, destroy his possessions, and rob Job of all his wealth, to turn his friends and even his wife against him. But Job had no inkling of what was going on in the center of heaven.

Job might have tried the seven sure steps for guidance. That sounds like the kind of advice his friends might have suggested. They did accuse him of sinning. But even with their meditation and great wisdom, they never really grasped the true events.

God hid himself from Job, and his silence lasted a long time. Eventually God spoke again. And, interestingly, the Lord didn't explain his silence to the patriarch.

Perhaps that's why it's hard when we encounter *Deus Absconditus* (an old theological phrase for the "God who hides himself"). We're programed to expect answers and explanations from the Divine Mind, almost as if he owed it to us. But God owes us nothing—not even constant direction.

At times, God may appear to be the hidden God; it may seem as though the silence of heaven mutely accuses us. But silence doesn't mean God has turned from us, or that sin has to reign in our lives.

Five years ago, God went mute on me. For at least three months—nothing. I couldn't sense God showing response to my prayers. It had been my custom to submit decisions to the Lord. While I didn't always get thunder and sparks of lightning, at least I received *something*, usually a sense of rightness about the situation. Or circumstances would indicate I was headed in the right direction. But during those months, even for the smallest matter, no answer came.

I searched my heart. Memories of past failures overwhelmed me. I then determined not to concentrate on them; after all, God had forgiven my past. "Lord, I'm not going to keep worrying about half a dozen things in which I might be wrong or still have the hint of sin in my life. I throw everything on you. If there's any place where I'm failing, cleanse me."

Nothing. Then I remembered that, a few years after my conversion to Christ, I had gone through a similar experience. For months, no guidance had seemed to be in evidence. And I had grown discouraged.

When I finally moved through that experience, I had determined that, if it ever occurred again, I would simply hold on until God reappeared.

The second time it happened, as I started to feel discouraged, I cried out, "Lord, I've experienced enough of your closeness and guidance in the past that I know you're there. I'm going to stick it out. When problems come up, I'll continue praying for guidance. I'll give you a chance to speak. And, if you don't, I'll just go on anyway until you open heaven again."

The days dragged on. I prayed, but still no guidance. I made decisions the best way I could—even a couple of important ones.

And then one day I was asking for his will about starting a new kind of outreach program. As I prayed, I felt as though the Lord spoke and said "No." I made no further plans.

Two days later, one of the leaders of the proposed plan called, "I haven't felt right about this. I think we ought to drop it."

It felt so good to hear God speak again.

I've talked to others who have gone for weeks, even months, with heavenly silence. But they also persisted. And one day they heard from God again.

I think of the story of Jacob. He fled from his father, whose blessing he had stolen, and from his brother, whom he had cheated. One night he slept in a barren field. In a dream he saw angels ascending and descending from heaven. He heard God speak. "I am the Lord, the God of Abraham your father and the God of Isaac; the land on which you lie I will give to you and to your descendants; and your descendants shall be like the dust of the earth, and you shall spread abroad to the west and to the east and to the north and to the south; and by you and your descendants shall all the families of the earth bless themselves" (Gen. 28:13–14). Then God said the best word of all to that fugitive, "Behold, I am with you and will keep you wherever you go, and will bring you back to this land; for I will not leave you until I have done that of which I have spoken to you" (v. 15).

The biblical account records that Jacob awakened and said, "Surely the Lord is in this place; and I did not know it" (v. 16). That's the message we need when we don't hear from God. God's always present, even when we don't know it.

We all encounter spiritual dry periods in our lives, *but they pass*. They pass just as the mountain peak experiences do. And one thing we can bear in mind: God is with us, regardless of how we feel about it.

So what do we do when God shuts off his end of the transmitting system?

Hold on.

As God said in Isaiah, "For a moment I hid my face from you." But it's only a temporary disruption. We wait until he transmits again. We continue walking by our faith, knowing that God cares and that he won't let us go astray.

I can't explain why God doesn't always respond to our prayers. Rather than complaining about his silence, perhaps we ought to be more thankful that he answers at all!

This much we know: when he becomes the hidden God, the situation is only temporary. He'll soon speak again!

16.

That's My Desire

An ancient theologian ₍or so *I remember from seminary days)* took a position on the will of God that went something like this: if I strongly desire to go one way, then obviously God's will lies in the opposite direction.

He heavily emphasized what theologians call the doctrine of total depravity, or humankind's fallen nature. That is, all of us, being sinful creatures, have turned away from God. Psalm 14 shouts it; Paul quotes it liberally in Romans 3. All this convinces us that none of us chooses the good, none of us seeks after God, none of us is without sin.

Some theological circles have put so much emphasis on our wayward natures that they disavow the idea of God's will ever merging with our own desires. How can we, as terrible sinners, ever want to do anything right or holy? We please God only by constantly overcoming our natural tendency to defy him. They've even pointed out that the perfect Son of man taught us this. God willed Jesus to die on the cross, but the Lord prayed for God to let "the cup" (i.e., suffering) pass him by. We, being corrupt by nature, they conclude, are even more prone to dodge God's will.

However, I've decided to argue with that theologian and his followers. I don't deny our spiritual depravity, or that we are, as Paul calls us, "sons of disobedience" (Eph. 3:2). But I also believe we can view ourselves from another perspective. As Christians we're God's people. We have, to use another biblical concept, the Holy Spirit indwelling us. He has "imparted" to us the divine nature. We're in the process of transformation, becoming more Christlike all the time.

This leads me to believe that God uses my own inclinations in guiding my life. Because I'm his child, I now have his nature maturing in me. He gets hold of my desires and uses them in guiding me, not in fighting me. Why not think of it like this: instead of God's being always out to break us, why can't he use our natures (which includes our desires, talents, and training) to accomplish his purpose? I believe he does!

Those words come as a reversal from what we frequently hear in the church. It's certainly different from what I assumed when I was first learning about God's will. I grew into the Christian faith believing that, in every situation needing guidance, we first emptied ourselves of preference. That was always step number one.

Seeking God's will meant prayers—deep, heart-searching, agonizing ones. But as long as we had any personal desires in the matter, we couldn't discern God's direction. Our wills blocked him.

"Not my will but thine" had to be the seminal statement before embarking on any course of seeking. Once we emptied ourselves of preference (and I'm not always sure that we did), we could begin hearing the Spirit speak. Sometimes we realized our biases, acknowledged that we couldn't quite lay them aside, and finally prayed, "God, despite the fact that I want this promotion, please destroy my preference. I want only your will. Help me not to want the promotion—only the will of God."

We sounded religious in our praying. We were also very sincere. And I'm not suggesting it's entirely wrong to pray that way. My objection is that it presents God's will from a negative viewpoint. We teach that God has to break through, that the process of hearing God's directions becomes a battle of our wills versus the Divine will. It implies that we're so far away from God's voice, it's almost impossible to know what he wants.

Let's try a different perspective.

Consider this: God made each of us unique. For instance, certain people have sunny dispositions. No matter how severe their problems in life, they bounce back quickly. Others, who seem to have easy lives with few problems, crumble over minor irritations.

Over the centuries, thinkers have tried to push people into categories. Some have listed eight basic types, others four. A few years ago, we stuck people into two major categories: introverts and extroverts. But no matter how we figure it, no one completely fits into those rigid typings. Why? Because no one fits the total picture. Each of us is slightly different from the others.

A more recent categorization of people is to class their behavior as Type A and Type B. Basically, the Type-A person is compulsive, time-oriented, always hurried and harried. We stamp Type-B labels on easygoing, procrastinating types. But again, no one totally fits either category.

Why don't we think of ourselves as unique, unable to be fully categorized? We take stock of ourselves, discover who we are and what we want, then seek the guidance of the Lord for our needs and our personalities.

Sounds simple. If I went to many counselors asking for help in choosing a vocation, here's how they'd assess me. They'd give me personality and preference tests, profiles, and I.Q. tests. From these, the experts would predict areas in which I'd be happy and effective in my life's work.

But somehow, when we start praying for God's will in specific instances, we throw out everything we've learned from the field of human behavior. It becomes simply a matter of seeking God's will out of the vacuum (remember, we cast aside personal preferences).

Here's how I came to this attitude. For a period of about two years, I went through a great deal of soul-searching about my future. Our church had awakened to the truth that we, a middle-class, white congregation, were now surrounded by a black population. After initial attempts to integrate blacks into our fellowship, we decided to close our doors, turn our facilities over to a black church, and let the members disperse. I believe we made the right decision.

But, in the midst of all that, I thought about me. What was my future? The members could simply join another church.

What did I want to do? Become pastor of another church? Leave the pastorate? Go back to teaching? For a long time I thought about my marketable skills, as I continued praying daily for God's guidance.

One day, I realized that I had three things I enjoyed doing above everything else: (1) preaching, (2) teaching, and (3) writing. I knew that, whatever I did with the rest of my life, I'd not feel content until those three yearnings found satisfaction. God's will for me included those three areas.

I considered teaching full time in the public schools (I had done that years ago), preaching on Sundays, and writing in my spare time, but somehow that didn't feel right. I envisioned myself working in the secular world in the field of personnel training. A dozen other ideas came and left. Nothing quite suited me except being a full-time pastor.

Eventually I went to another church (where I am now in my seventh year). I received distinct guidance from the Lord to accept that call; I know the Holy Spirit led me here. Almost as important, however, is the fact that God's will fits my own desire.

Instead of subjugating and pushing aside my own likes and dislikes, I'm now looking at God's will through those desires. Doing this helps me eliminate many possibilities.

For example, I don't like strict nine-to-five hours. I've worked under those conditions, but I do better by setting my own hours and giving the work my best efforts when I'm feeling my best. I do most of my writing before nine in the morning or after nine at night. In addition, I've discovered that I can only spend about half a day in the office. After that, I find reasons to visit people, run errands, or jog six miles. I've since adjusted my schedule so that, if I have appointments or counseling sessions in the morning, I'm out jogging or visiting people in the afternoons. This fits my nature, and I feel my lifestyle pleases God.

I remember, however, that in late 1973, when I went through the period of reassessment, I didn't hear often from heaven. Perhaps I was grieving too much over the future of the church. For me, as for others, preparing to die as a congregation brought deep pain.

I prayed for guidance. When the Lord chose not to speak or show me what to do, I felt a terrible void in my life. Questions such as, "Why no sense of divine guidance" troubled me. Then one morning I made a final commitment. I knelt by my bedside and talked to my Heavenly Father: "Lord, you know who I am. You know what I have to offer you and your church. I'm tired of agonizing and searching and deciding, only to find myself unhappy about my decisions. Please use me in whatever capacity you want."

A few days after praying that way—and really meaning it—a pulpit committee from Riverdale contacted me. I accepted the call, and have never had any regrets.

I may leave this church next year, or in ten years. But I know from that time of searching that I have three basic areas in my life that require fulfillment. Whatever the Lord has for me will satisfy those areas.

Even beyond the matter of major calling, such as our life's work, the principle still applies. God uses our desires. He knows what gets us excited. He uses our personalities and our make-ups to guide our lives.

Think of God's wisdom. He takes our basic preferences, molds them, and uses them to do his work. We don't have to deny our inclinations or apologize for them.

God will lead us *through* our desires—not *in spite* of them.

17.

That Inner Certainty

"I simply knew," she said.

"But how?" I persisted.

Mom Brackett fumbled for words after that. "I—I can't explain. I simply knew."

Her answer baffled me. I had been a Christian approximately a year when my wife's mother, Cornelia Brackett, said those words. She had changed her membership from a church she had attended for twenty years. Although it was a church with a membership of nearly a thousand, she had been active and knew everyone. Now she had begun attending a congregation with fewer than seventy-five people.

"But how did you know the Lord wanted you to make the change?" She knew I wasn't trying to talk her out of her decision. I was struggling to understand how the Lord had led Mom.

"Cec, I have the Holy Spirit. I know he guides me. Sometimes I stumble with decisions. And at times I make decisions or choices and I don't really know what God wants. But once in awhile . . ."—she paused for an extraordinarily long time—"but once in awhile, I know. There's that inner knowledge. I don't have any proof. I don't have anything I can point to. It's a certainty, and no one can talk me out of it."

"I wish I could experience that kind of certain leading from the Lord," I replied.

And over the years I *have* experienced it. Not regularly. Not often. But it has come. And, like Mom Brackett, when it happens *I know*. I hear no angelic voices, no hallelujah choruses nor fire alarms. I see no verses of Scripture flashing. But there is a quiet, inner certainty.

How does one go about explaining that kind of spiritual guidance from the Lord? I've decided I can't explain it. Perhaps that's what makes it mysterious, exciting, unusual, and extraordinary. The best I can do in this chapter is to *share* the experience of this inner witness, then offer a few conclusions on this form of spiritual leading.

I can think of two distinct times in my life when the Holy Spirit gave me such an inward conviction that nothing could have dissuaded me. The first happened in 1957.

At the time I was taking summer courses at a Chicago college. While walking one summer afternoon in the business district, I recall looking up at a theater marquee and seeing the name of the then-showing film, "Tanganyika." I gave the sign only a casual glance, but I suddenly had an inner assurance that I was going there. Tanganyika (later called Tanzania) was one of the places where we worked in Africa. In fact, the mission station where we lived for nearly four years was less than ten miles from the Tanzania border.

That day in Chicago no lights flashed. I had no great emotional experience. There was simply the certainty that God wanted me to be a missionary in Africa. Although three years passed before we actually went, I knew that God had called me.

The second experience of this inner witness occurred during our last year in Africa. We had stayed beyond our regular term of service. I had no immediate plans. I had thought vaguely about returning to school for graduate studies, and had written a couple of schools for information.

One day, I read a copy of a British religious magazine. The back page contained an announcement of an American professor speaking at one of the British churches. It listed him as a professor at Columbia Theological Seminary in Decatur, Georgia.

Neither the school nor the location meant anything to me, but as I read the name of the school, I felt that inner witness again! It was as though a voice said, "That's where I want you to go." I didn't understand the experience, but I didn't doubt it.

In both those instances, it never occurred to me to question. The Lord had spoken. We began packing our goods, making plans to return to America—even before I received a letter of acceptance from the seminary.

I recall telling another missionary of my future plans. He asked if I had been officially accepted. "Not yet," I replied.

"Then why are you doing all this?" He saw boxes of my books stacked and covering one wall of the living room. "Shouldn't you wait until you've heard? They might not want you."

I remember laughing, "They'll take me. They may not even know it, but they will."

And they did.

Linda Weller, secretary of Fayette Presbyterian Church, shared an incident with me. A man, in town for only one day, had to find a place for his aged mother to live. She was being evicted, and had no other relatives.

The man, asking the pastor, David Black, for help, told him the whole sad story. Linda, who was in the office, also heard. Without any conscious thought, she replied, "Take her to Christian City. That's the place for her."

Christian City had only recently announced the opening of a convalescence center, and had said that they would eventually open a section for apartment-type living. Linda had not heard that the apartments were even open. But the certainty of her own words made her know they were.

Linda grabbed the phone, called a friend at Christian City. The woman replied, "We're having our grand opening today. If you'll get the son here right now, I'll get his mother in. If you wait beyond today, she'll have to add her name to a long waiting list."

The son rushed over, arranged for his mother's transfer, and left the city—all in less than twenty-four hours. Linda, in relating this, said, "As soon as those words popped out of my mouth, I knew it was right. I couldn't have told you *how* I knew."

Another incident involved my friend Terry. He was sitting in a mission's conference his church sponsored. For several months he had been seeking guidance for his life, although the search had not reached an acute stage. "As a layman from Brazil spoke in an evening service," Terry said, "I knew—instantly—God wanted me in Brazil. I can't tell you how I knew, only that it was clear and irrefutable."

After sharing several instances of this inner guidance from the Holy Spirit, let's make a few conclusions:

First, I believe it's a rare experience. I say this not only because it has happened to me so infrequently, but because others have said the same thing. Many fine Christians have never had such an experience. Others speak of it as one of the awesome, significant spiritual highpoints in life.

Gus shared the following experience with me. He said, "It was such a powerful moment in my life, I've not shared it with more than half a dozen people since it happened twenty years ago."

Gus had been planning to visit friends, but got lost. He had no idea where he was, and seemed to be driving through a maze of rambling roads and dead-end streets. He kept thinking he'd find some street that looked familiar. Then, as he approached a four-way stop, something happened. Gus described it this way: "I heard a voice—probably in my head—but a voice that said 'Turn left.'"

"I knew that was the direction to turn, although I had no idea where I was. I went left, drove another two or three blocks, and suddenly arrived at their house. Just as I pulled into the driveway, another car was getting ready to pull out. My friends introduced me to the other driver. We started talking, and, an hour later, the man offered me a job, which I badly needed. It's the only time in life that I recall having such an absolute certainty about anything."

Second, it sounds very much like the promise of Isaiah 65:24: "Before they call, I will answer; and while they are yet speaking, I will hear." When it does happen, it's as though God had anticipated our need and provided an answer either before we asked or almost as soon as we became aware of the predicament.

Third, because it's unusual, it comes with greater certainty. As I look in the Bible and read of God's appearing in human form, he made it clear who he was and what he intended. Those to whom he appeared expressed no doubts.

Joshua, for instance, just before fighting for control of the promised land, encountered a military-looking man who said, "'As commander of the army of the Lord I have now come.' Joshua fell on his face to the earth, and worshiped, then said to him, 'What does my Lord bid his servant?' And the commander of the Lord's army said to Joshua, 'Put off your shoes from your feet; for the place where you stand is holy.' And Joshua did so" (Josh. 5:14–15). Joshua *knew*—he was in the presence of God.

Finally, I don't think it's an experience to seek for. When it happens, it's because God intervenes in the normal affairs of life.

I've heard those who have known this unique experience say, "People don't always understand." And because it's hard for some people to understand, those who have gone through it often feel reluctant to speak of their experience.

I'm not concerned about more people experiencing that inner certainty, only that we be open to it in our own lives and in the lives of others.

18.

People Guiders

A part of me still lives in Africa, even though it's been a dozen years since we left. In fact, not more than ten days have passed in which I've not thought about Kenya. Probably my love for the people and the land will never completely disappear.

A few months ago both Shirley and I seriously considered returning to the mission field. We prayed about it several days, submitted an application to the mission board, and even talked with the head of personnel for our denomination. We were not too old, even to go to a new country. Shirley's problem with arthritis would not be a holdback. It appeared as though the Lord might be reopening the door and saying to us, once again, "Go."

We shared our burden with several friends, and we received a mixed reaction. Bob said, "We need more dedicated people. I hope it will work out." Another friend laughed, "You've done your bit; let someone else go." One friend, Maurice, said, "Cec, I know missions is heavy on your heart, but I don't believe God wants you back there. At least not now." And he was a missionary himself!

He explained several reasons why, in his thinking, God would use me more fully in this country. And when he finished, I could only nod and say, "You're right." He spoke to me as a messenger of the Lord.

That's one instance of the Holy Spirit using people to direct me. I don't think my missionary friend Maurice felt he was guiding me in the Lord's will. He was expressing an opinion, but, as he spoke, something inside me responded, "Yes! Yes!" And I knew that was the word of the Lord.

God has used other people to guide me. When it has happened, they didn't always realize they were being used by the Spirit.

This happened to me a few months after I became a pastor. I had always followed the accepted sermon tradition of having three major points with one illustration for each, and then closing with a hymn or poem. Occasionally I would share a personal experience—always a positive illustration.

One Sunday morning, at the end of the service and after most people had gone, I stepped away from the front door to grab a quick sip at the drinking fountain. As I bent over to sip, I overheard a woman say (she was in the restroom, but her voice carried clearly), "I enjoyed the service. But he's like all the others. I'm tired of hearing how good preachers can be. Don't they ever fail at anything? Don't they struggle like the rest of us? Do they always have just the right word to settle every situation?"

I didn't listen to any more—probably because I didn't want to. Inwardly I fumed at what the woman had said. Yet the more my mind dwelt on the matter, the more I realized she was right. I hadn't been fair to my congregation. They heard only of my victories. I determined that from then on I would be honest with them. They needed to know I didn't have God cornered, that I didn't have all the answers.

I don't know who that woman was, or if she ever came back. But I'll always be grateful for the guidance the Holy Spirit gave me through her. Since then, in my preaching and later in my writing, I've determined to present myself as a fellow struggler, not as Cec, the always-victorious one.

In that overheard remark, God used a human being as a messenger of his. I'm thankful.

God speaks through ordinary people and common situations. But he speaks especially when teachers and preachers present his Word. I wouldn't be an ordained minister if I didn't believe that. Not that each person hears exactly the word of guidance for every situation every time I open my mouth. But I believe God has chosen to speak through the Bible as it is proclaimed and explained to his people.

On a recent Sunday, I preached from 1 Kings 19. That's the story of Elijah. Fearful of Queen Jezebel, he fled into the wilderness. He lay down, after traveling all day, and moaned, "I've had enough. . . . Take away my life" (1 Kings 19:4, TLB). I called my sermon "Poor Little Me." In the message, I also pointed out that God finally told Elijah to get up and get back to work. He wasn't the only one who served God, as he had complained; seven thousand men of Israel remained loyal.

At the end of that service, three different people said almost the same thing to me: "I needed to hear that. Sometimes I get so wrapped up in my own problems, I think of no one else. I even think that maybe God is against me."

I know the Lord used my preaching that morning. One woman who heard the message has remarked on several occasions, "Everytime I start feeling down, I think of that sermon. I say to myself, 'Okay, poor little me, get up and get moving again.'"

I also believe in the ministry of professional counseling. Some people have a gift from God that I marvel at. They listen to people tell their stories. They seem to know exactly what to say and which questions to ask. These gifted people often seem to give guidance from God without any apparent effort. It's as though the words flow naturally from them.

I have no great ability to counsel, and certainly no gift in that area. But a recent experience stands out in my mind. Len and his fiance had broken up six weeks before their wedding. He, brokenhearted and depressed, came to my office. Hardly realizing what I was saying, I asked, "Len, are you upset because she's broken your heart, or is it more a sense of personal loss to your self-esteem because you've not been able to hold on to her?" I have no idea why I said those words, and nothing in his conversation had indicated such an attitude.

He stared at me for a long time. Then he said, "You know, you're right. I don't think I really wanted to marry her. I didn't want to lose her either. You've really hit the nail on the head."

That was the beginning of Len's victory over his depression. While this experience happens to me rarely, God often uses people with such gifts to guide his people.

I also believe in the principle of Proverbs 15:22: "Without

counsel plans go wrong, but with many advisors they succeed." In our church we have a board of elders. While we allow each committee on that board a lot of freedom, we expect them to bring the big decision-making issues to the entire board. Many times I've been convinced that I knew the solution to the situation before the board met.

As I've listened, I've realized that someone else had the word of the Lord. If the board had simply said, "Okay, Cec, just do it your way and we'll go along," the whole situation might have proven disastrous.

At the same time, of course, I've been able to give the word of the Lord to the board of elders. They've listened, accepted my ideas, and events have proved I was right. But more often, we hear the voice of the Lord together. And we're not often conscious at the time that God is speaking to us.

Acts 13:1–2 declares that prophets and teachers prayed in Antioch and "the Holy Spirit said, 'Set apart for me Barnabas and Saul for the work to which I have called them.'" Possibly one of the prophets stood up and pronounced a thus-saith-the-Lord message. But I wonder if it did not come about that, after they had prayed, fasted, and thought the matter through sufficiently, all of them sensed Paul and Barnabas were the men to send. No one knows the answer, of course. But it seems more the way in which God works.

I am convinced of the validity of God's working through the human agency. But I don't think everyone has the word of guidance—even when they may think they do! Haven't we all had well-meaning Christian friends who have said, "Now, here's what you need to do"?

I remember when Shirley and I dated. A well-intentioned minister, convinced we were not suited to each other, not only advised Shirley against the marriage, but even proposed to have her date another eligible man he knew. His advice was well-intentioned, but we both knew he was wrong, and we married. And we know it was God's will for us.

How do we know when God speaks to us through other people? We can't always be absolutely certain, but I have a few suggestions on this:

1. *Be open to God.* Let him have the opportunity to speak through any medium he wants. When someone offers a suggestion, don't wipe it out of your mind or put it into action until you've prayed about it, thought about it, and it feels right.

2. *I say "feels right" because it has to have the right ring to it.* Some call it an inner witness of the spirit. When the word comes, a voice within says, "Yes, I agree." But I'm reluctant to act on anyone's advice until first I'm comfortable with it.

3. *A third suggestion: share it with some of your Christian friends.* Tell them your dilemma. Ask for their prayers. I have several people I can ask to pray with me about almost any matter. They may tell me what they feel, but they sincerely pray for the Lord's directions to me.

As I think of the Bible, it's no surprise that God calls people guiders into service today. That's always been his pattern. Remember Joseph advising Pharaoh? Moses laid down the Ten Commandments, but he also advised the people and settled disputes. When it finally became too much for him, he delegated the advising and guiding chore to seventy leaders of the nation.

Throughout the Old Testament, the Spirit raised up men (and a few women) who said boldly, "Thus says the Lord." New Testament voices speak just as strongly.

I don't care *how* God leads me. His directions for my daily living are the primary concern. His methods are secondary.

And you know what? Just think, *today* you might be a divine messenger yourself. Today the Spirit might give you a word that's exactly what a troubled soul waits to hear. So the fact that God speaks through people lays a double challenge on us—to hear God speak through others, but also to be an instrument through whom God speaks his will!

19.

Two or Three Others

We had finished our business, and our board was getting ready to dismiss, when Ralph asked for permission to speak. "I want to see an evening service here at our church. We've never had one as long as I've been a member, and I think we need it. I change shifts, and I want a service to attend when I can't get here on Sunday morning."

"I feel the same way," Joe called out from the back of the room.

Within a matter of minutes, we decided to have Sunday evening worship, something that had not been done in our church for many years. The services have since grown from a handful to fifty or sixty people.

Actually, I had been thinking of such a service. But I had only been the pastor for two months and hesitated to initiate too many changes. I didn't know the members well enough to have any idea of how they'd respond. Knowing that most Presbyterians don't have the habit of attending evening activities, I assumed it would be a less-attended service. And, as pastor, I didn't need more work.

But I had envisioned another service at our church, one in which people would have a higher level of participation. When Ralph and Joe both insisted on the additional worship opportunity, I knew the Lord was guiding.

That experience and others which followed have led me to rediscover an important verse in the Old Testament:

106

A single witness shall not prevail against a man for any crime or for any wrong in connection with any offense that he has committed; only on the evidence of two witnesses, or of three witnesses, shall a charge be sustained (Deut. 19:15).

The meaning of the verse appears obvious. When someone charged another with a crime, the verdict could not be decided by one person's word against another. God said that two or three people would have to testify against the accused.

This commandment about two or three witnesses appears not only throughout the Old Testament, but in the New as well (see Matt. 18:16, 2 Cor. 13:1, John 8:17, 1 Tim. 5:19, Heb. 10:18). In each reference, the same intent is evident: whenever any question of guilt arose, the testimony of one person could not convict. It took a second eyewitness, or even a third.

I go into detail because I'm quite aware of the specific intent of Deuteronomy 19:15. But for me it has also come to be, by application, a means of discovering God's will.

For instance, when I've been uncertain about a plan of action, this is one method I have relied on heavily, although I don't simply fasten onto the concept of two or three witnesses and then make it the sole principle for guidance.

I began to use this method as a result of several experiences.

I've already mentioned the Sunday evening services. Approximately a year later, I began feeling concerned about small-group relationships. I felt (as I still do) that Christians need to be part of the total life of a congregation. But every Christian also needs a small group of individuals with whom to share. These relationships come about in many ways—through choir membership, through active participation in a Sunday school class, even through playing softball or basketball.

I believe people need some kind of group within the church in which they can open themselves up to others, a place or group about which they can say, "These folks understand me. They know my weaknesses and still love me."

Why not midweek prayer or Bible study in homes? I wondered. Having it in homes would keep it informal and provide the opportunity for people to sit around in a face-to-face situation.

One Sunday evening, before I had talked to anyone about the idea, a lovely lady named Mary Carter said to me, "Cec, have you thought about having some kind of prayer group in the homes? I need that kind of fellowship. And my home is open if you want it."

I don't remember exactly how I answered, but something to the effect of "Let's pray about it." Within a week, two other people, Stan and Donna, each independent of the other, had proposed the same idea. Two weeks later we started home groups.

Still another similar situation occurred before I began sensing a divine principle at work. This one affected my writing. I had been having some success in writing, and I was loving it. Then I wondered about writing fiction. I tried a few fiction pieces, but when they didn't sell I assumed that was not what I was meant to do.

One day a novelist (who is also a Christian) read some articles I had written. "Cec, I think you ought to try to stretch yourself. You need to attempt fiction as well."

I thanked her, but took no steps in that direction. Six months later, I taught nonfiction writing for the Dixie Council of Authors and Journalists Workshop. Ruth Tucker Herbert, the fiction instructor, sat in on one of my classes. The next day, she said, "You must write fiction. I want to see you write a religious novel. And I know you can do it!"

It had happened again! First my own desire emerging, followed by two separate witnesses, with whom I had not shared my thoughts. As soon as this book is completed, my next project is to write fiction.* I believe that's God's Spirit leading me.

Using the principle of two or three witnesses as a means of discerning guidance makes sense to me. The fact that it distorts the obvious meaning of the text is no problem, because there's an implied principle, even from Deuteronomy 19:15: when questions lurk, let two or three people give their witness before you act. Make no serious decisions on the opinion or testimony of one person.

As I've watched this operating in my life, I have seen that each

---

*Since writing this chapter, I have completed and sold two religious novels.

time these witnesses have come to me *unsolicited*. The various instances were usually preceded by prayer and uncertainty. Then the witnesses came to me, almost as if I had asked.

This happened again only recently. One morning, sitting at my desk, I realized I had not seen Rodney at services for several weeks. I prayed about whether to contact him or not. But since it was mid-July, I thought, "Perhaps he's on vacation."

Not more than ten minutes later, the phone rang. Anne, one of our sharpest members, had several things on her mind. Then, just before hanging up, she said, "Have you heard from Rodney lately? I haven't seen him around. Wonder if we ought to give him a call?"

Later that day, Skip breezed through the office and, among other things, commented, "I haven't seen Rodney since the start of the softball season. Do you know what's happened to him?"

"No, I don't know. But it's strange; I was thinking about him myself." That evening I called him on the phone.

After several minutes of talk he said, "I've been going through a terrible time of depression lately [he had been divorced a few months earlier]. I had begun to wonder if anyone from the church cared. Your calling me today helps me know differently. I had decided that if I didn't hear from someone at the church this week, I wouldn't be back again."

I silently thanked the Lord for the prodding of two other people!

Through my own experiences, I have come to the conclusion that "the evidence of two . . . or of three witnesses" represents a bona fide means of ascertaining God's will.

Let's distill a few operating principles from these experiences:

1. *The voices of two or three witnesses come as just that—witnesses.* That is, they don't bring the initial word of the Lord. They *confirm*. They become the backup squad. It's almost as though God says, "Cec didn't quite grasp the message when I spoke directly to him. I'll send a couple of messengers to help him know he heard right."

2. *The two or three witnesses provide assurance.* In both the matter of the Sunday evening services and that of starting home groups, I would have been hesitant to take the first steps, if I hadn't been assured of God's leading. The same ideas coming

from independent sources provided that assurance. I had not talked previously to Ralph or Joe about the evening services. I had no inkling that anyone else in the congregation felt the way I did.

3. *The two or three witnesses give the courage to take risks.* Who is perfect in faith? We all struggle at times, not quite able to make a decision or to begin an action. Questions jump at us: "But what if it doesn't work?" Getting the nudge from those outside voices enables me to take the leap of faith.

This method doesn't constitute a primary source for knowing God's directions. It becomes a helpful device that he uses from time to time. I not only get excited when I think of the Lord prompting two other people to speak to me, but I rejoice just knowing that God wants to direct my life.

As I finish this, I recall an incident back in my seminary days. I had not thought of writing, other than the normal number of academic papers. On the bulletin board one day, the seminary listed opportunities to compete for prizes on Honors Day. I hurriedly read the notice and thought about it for a few seconds. Then I remembered that the awards the previous years had gone to seniors, and I was only in my middle year of seminary. I wanted to enter, but didn't think I had a chance.

A friend, Jerry, who was standing next to me, said, "Cec, you're going to enter a paper, aren't you?" I don't recall my answer, just that I was noncommittal.

Later that day, another classmate said to me, "Did you see that thing up about papers for Honors Day? You ought to enter."

My two friends' words provided the impetus. I submitted a paper to each of the three categories. On Honors Day I won first prize in one field, and second in another. I wouldn't even have submitted if my two classmates hadn't spoken to me.

Considering the concept of two or three witnesses encourages me. Think of it—the Lord cares enough to make sure we get the message! It's not just a grab-it-now-or-never approach. He speaks. Then he confirms.

Each time I discover God's will confirmed to me by two or three others, I usually have only one word to say to the Lord— *thanks.*

"Thanks, Lord, for caring that much!"

20.

Led By the Spirit

The morning started with a jangling telephone call. And then another. And another. Four people had to see me "right now," and by midafternoon I still had three hospital calls to make.

Instead of hurrying from the office, I sat quietly at my desk, breathing deeply and trying to relax. "Lord, I've run at top speed all day. The harder I work, the more I seem *not* to get done. A dozen things are pulling at me right now, and I hardly know what to do next." Then I prayed, "Lord, lead me by your Spirit." I relaxed another minute or two, and then started to get up.

Call Tom.

I didn't hear a voice. It was only an inner urging. "Why should I call Tom?" I asked myself. He's a friend, but I had no special reason to call him. And in the midst of my busy schedule, I didn't have time for social calls!

Call Tom.

That inner urging persisted. I must have argued with myself a full minute. Finally I dialed his number. He answered before the first ring was completed. "Tom, I'm not even sure why I'm calling. Your name just kept coming to me and—"

"I know why you called," he answered. "I was sitting here, even had my hand on the phone. I was praying, 'I need to talk to someone, God. Please show me whom.'"

I call that experience "being led by the Spirit." I believe it's that kind of sensitivity to God's Spirit that the apostle Paul meant when he wrote, "For all who are led by the Spirit of God are sons of God" (Rom. 8:14).

I wish this experience of my being in tune with the Spirit and responding to Tom's need formed part of every day's experience. It doesn't—at least not for me. But that, along with other moments of being in touch with the Holy Spirit, convinces me that it's a goal to reach for. As I learn to respond to the Spirit's urgings, surely it can become a more frequent experience. And I'm trying to become more sensitive to the divine impulse at work.

I also think of a somewhat similar experience with Margie, a middle-aged almost-invalid who had had her toes amputated, and was battling several other physical problems. Every once in awhile I'd feel a strong urge to see Margie. The first time it happened, I was fairly close to her house, so I drove up and knocked on the door. When she laboriously walked to the door, opened it, and saw me, she smiled and said, "Thank you, Lord."

After I got inside she said, "I was praying this afternoon. I kept saying, 'Lord, I know how busy Cec is. But I need him. And if you agree that I need him, please have him come over or at least give me a phone call.' And you came!"

Sometimes I hear the voice of the Lord—not literally hear it, of course. But I have an inner sense of divine prompting. I'm learning to obey that prompting.

At other times I simply don't know when God speaks. That's why I've set as one of my spiritual goals, being constantly in touch with the Holy Spirit for his leading in my life. I'm not asking God to show me visions every hour, or to let me hear voices from heaven, or to let me feel angels' wings flapping. But I do want to learn how to be led by the Spirit.

Sometimes I've missed the Lord's directions, too. On one occasion, as I drove two blocks from Steve's house, I felt an urge to drop in and see him. *Ah, he's probably still at work*, I said to myself. *And anyway, I've got so much to do.*

On Sunday Steve came to church. "A couple of days ago I went through a bad time. I lost my job. I had a fight with my wife, and she almost left me. I started to call you. Wish I had. I'm okay now, but it's been a couple of rough days." As he poured out his story, I realized it had been the same afternoon!

Because I've both enjoyed the blessing of being led by the Spirit and mourned my insensitivity to his prompting, I'm reaching out for the Holy Spirit to lead my life. As I've thought about it, I've come to believe that one mark of Christian maturity is being led by the Spirit. In the Bible it's the difference between being a *child* and a *son*.

Romans 8:14 says it best, but it's not the only place. Other verses show the same distinction between infancy and maturity. John 1:12 says that when we come to Christ we become children. Peter exhorts us that, as newborns, we should desire spiritual milk.

In another place, the apostle Paul rebukes the Corinthians, saying that they're still spiritual babies, unable to eat meat, able only to handle milk. Hebrews 5:12–14 reads: "For though by this time you ought to be teachers, you need some one to teach you again the first principles of God's word. You need milk, not solid food; for every one who lives on milk is unskilled in the word of righteousness, for he is a child. But solid food is for the mature, for those who have their faculties trained by practice to distinguish good from evil."

All these verses tell us that God never intends for us to remain like newborns all our lives. Part of the goal for Christians is to grow. And one of those marks of spiritual growth is being led by the Spirit: "For all who are led by the Spirit of God, are sons of God" (Rom. 8:14).

We move forward. We're not content being the same person we were ten years ago. Or, to use Paul's analogy, a son of God is led by the Spirit; a child doesn't understand and obey. A son *knows*; a child *wonders*. A son moves ahead in faith; a child holds back. A son declares, "God speaks," and a child asks, "Does he?"

Everyone born of God belongs to God. But the terms *son* and *child* distinguish the spiritual development. Naturally, only God really makes the distinction and knows when one enters the realm of sonship, but it remains an encouragement for our moving forward.

My wife once felt troubled over Romans 8:14 and other verses about spiritual maturity. She especially wanted to know how to hear the voice of the Lord. One morning she was reading the tenth chapter of John's gospel in which Jesus talked about himself as the Good Shepherd and about his people as sheep. In one place (v. 3) he says, "The sheep hear his voice, and he calls his own sheep by name and leads them out." In the same chapter, the Lord said, "I know my own and my own know me" (v. 14).

As Shirley meditated, she asked, "Lord, how is that? You say your sheep know your voice. That means they follow your leading. I'm a Christian and I love you. Yet sometimes I don't know when it's your voice."

She says that a thought suddenly surged through her mind: *sheep* know the voice; *lambs* have to learn.

That's how I view the secret of being led by the Spirit—it's a learning process. No one comes by it easily or automatically. We begin by committing ourselves to Jesus Christ. From there we learn to listen, to seek, to obey.

I can't give infallible rules for being led by the Spirit. I don't even experience that constant guidance myself. But as I grope and grow, I have learned a few things, which I pass on to you:

1. *We draw upon our past experiences.* I think back to how the Spirit led me in the cases of Tom and Margie. I also recall how the Spirit tried to lead me to Steve's house. As I become aware of how that voice speaks and has spoken in the past, it becomes something for me to rely upon in the future. I learn to distinguish God's voice from the myriad of sounds around me.

I learned the importance of distinguishing sounds when we first went to Africa as missionaries. We had expected to work among a particular tribe, and had learned some Swahili so we could communicate. Then, a short time before leaving for Kenya, we received the official message: "You are going to work among the Luo tribe. You will learn Luo."

That particular tribe did have the Bible translated (although the Old Testament was done poorly), but since few white people knew the language, we had few books to assist us. We had to learn from the nationals themselves.

The first two weeks I could not distinguish one word from another. All conversation sounded like one long word to me. Then one African who spoke English agreed to teach us Luo. At the end of the first lesson I realized I was already able to hear specific words—not everything, but the few words that he had taught us. Then I learned a few more words. In time, we were speaking, hearing, communicating, and even thinking in the local dialect. I recall thinking (after we had been in the country several months), "Why did it take me so long to learn Luo?"

Learning to speak Luo was a process. Over a period of six months, I learned to listen intently to what Africans said. As I grew more fluent it took less concentration. One day I realized that, in my private prayers, I had been thinking and praying in the Luo tongue. Then I knew I had learned the language.

That's how I see our learning the leading of the Holy Spirit. It's a process. We make mistakes. We keep at it. We concentrate on listening. But we also rely upon our past experiences to guide us in our future expectations.

2. *Use common sense.* Often we think of guidance as something that comes out of the blue heavens. But the longer I walk with Jesus Christ, the more I realize that common sense is one of the voices by which he speaks.

When I say common sense, I'm referring not only to the things that are logical and practical, but also to things that are reasonable. God may transcend this level, but that's often where he works and how he leads us.

3. *Expect God's guidance.* A mark of spiritual maturity is realizing that God will lead. It's an inner assurance that God cares what happens and will enable us to solve our difficulties.

On one occasion, while I was in graduate school, my family faced a crisis. We needed money for extensive car repairs (a common crisis for us in those days). I shared the problem with the children as we began our devotional time together. It had been a hard month for us financially. My spirits sagged.

Cecile, our quiet one, looked at me and said, "But God will show us what to do." Just hearing her say those words gave me a tremendous boost. I knew the Lord would guide us. As it turned out, the mechanic who repaired the car, knowing I was in school, allowed me to pay in three installments with no interest. I'm grateful to him, but even more grateful for my then-young daughter who reminded me to expect God's guidance.

And God does lead us by his Spirit.

Sometimes he's simply waiting for us to give him the opportunity.

21.

Guidance Through Gifts

"The house is a mess. Laundry is scattered everywhere, and— but, yes, she can come," Bunny said. A woman needed a place to stay for at least one night. Did I have someone who would take her in? Bunny hardly hesitated before agreeing.

Good things came out of that incident. It provided an opportunity for the woman to see Christianity lived on a day-to-day basis. She also encountered a close husband-wife relationship in that home.

I wasn't surprised when Bunny agreed to take in the woman, nor was I surprised that everything worked out well. The Lord has given Bunny and Clark the gift of opening their home to others. When people enter that house, they no longer feel like strangers. The ability to make people feel comfortable and wanted is the gift of hospitality (see Romans 12:13). Not every Christian has that ability.

For years, most of us have been vaguely aware of passages in the Bible which mention spiritual gifts (*charismata* from the Greek root, *charis*). The major passages are 1 Corinthians 12 and 14, Ephesians 4, Romans 12:6–8, and 1 Peter 4:10–11. Other passages in the New Testament mention one or more of the gifts (see 1 Cor. 1:5–7; 13:1–3, 8–10; 2 Cor. 8:7; 1 Thess. 5:20; 1 Tim. 4:14; 2 Tim. 1:6–7; Heb. 2:4).

Yet even with all those references to *charismata*, until the mid-1970s hardly a book on spiritual gifts appeared in stores. The Pentecostal churches seemed the only ones who staked claims on those portions of the New Testament. But a new wave (perhaps a new awareness of the Holy Spirit) began sweeping across the church. Suddenly the major religious publishers, jumping in the water while the tide is still coming in, have brought out books on spiritual gifts.

While not agreeing in detail, these current writings all concur in recognizing *charismata* for God's church today. Most agree that the listings in the major Scripture references above do not provide the gamut of the gifts, but that they do suggest the wide range of God's dealings with his people.

Reading the various sections of the New Testament that mention spiritual gifts raises several questions. First, how many spiritual gifts does the Bible mention? The answer depends on how you interpret the passages, as well as whose book you read.

For instance, C. Peter Wagner, who identifies twenty-seven, lists *voluntary poverty* as a spiritual gift. He cites 1 Corinthians 13:3, "If I give away all I have. . . ." He defines this gift as the ability to renounce material comfort and to adopt a lifestyle at the poverty level in order to serve God effectively.

Rick Yohn identifies twenty gifts, one of them being the gift of music, which is not on Wagner's list. Kenneth Cain Kinghorn, also coming up with twenty, has variations on Yohn's list. Leslie B. Flynn's title tells his position: *Nineteen Gifts of the Spirit.* *

Probably more important than settling on the number of gifts is to ask, *what are spiritual gifts?* The answer: special abilities God gives his people to accomplish his work. These are not natural talents which we all have. Human talents, although from God, can function independently of the Holy Spirit. Spiritual gifts, however, operate by the special workings of the Holy Spirit. That's why the definition includes the words, "to accomplish his work."

Third, why talk about gifts? Knowing our spiritual giftedness enables us to be more in tune with God's will. As we become

---

*C. Peter Wagner, *Your Spiritual Gifts Can Help Your Church Grow* (Glendale, Calif.: Regal Books, 1979); Rick Yohn, *Discover Your Spiritual Gift* (Wheaton, Ill.: Tyndale House, 1977); Kenneth Cain Kinghorn, *Gifts of the Spirit* (Nashville, Tenn.: Abingdon, 1976); Leslie B. Flynn, *Nineteen Gifts of the Spirit* (Wheaton, Ill.: Victor Books, 1974).

aware of the spiritual talents the Spirit of God equips us with, not only do we want to use them, but they also give us directions on how to serve Jesus Christ.

I began an awareness of my own spiritual enablements during my seminary days (although I don't believe I used the words spiritual gifts). As part of the required program, all students did an internship at a hospital. Five of us chose the Central State Hospital in Georgia, a mental institution. Every Monday for one school term, we spent the entire day there. Mornings we would visit patients, and in the afternoons we would sit with supervisors, evaluating our experiences. On our first day, the supervisors assigned us to different areas. I went to the chronic ward.

On that ward, none of the approximately fifty patients had been there fewer than seventeen years. One thirty-five-year-old man had been confined since shortly after his eighteenth birthday. Because of the seriousness of the patients' problems, I resented my assignment at first. Several of the patients on the chronic ward could not speak. Few could carry on conversations. The other students went to areas where they met patients who were nearing release. They established relationships, and carried on normal conversations.

During my first day on the ward, while reading records, I overheard a nurse treating one of the patients curtly. As I listened, I became angry at the nurse. After the poor man had moved on, I finally said, "You talked to him as though he were some kind of stupid animal. He's a person, even if he's a sick one."

She smirked, "That's the way they understand. Talk to them like normal people, and they don't respond."

My anger intensified, although I said nothing more to her. In the afternoon, I shared this incident with the others. The chaplain-supervisor said, "Murphey, do you suppose you have a built-in empathy for the underdog?"

I don't recall the rest of the discussion, but as we drove back to the seminary I thought about his words. He had sized me up. That's also part of my approach to ministry. I feel deep compassion for hurting and outcast people. It's not a feeling I've worked for; it's an ability God has given me. It's part of what I recognize as my gift of pastoring (see Eph. 4:11). During those weeks, I developed a special feeling for those inmates. I knew many by name. The few that could talk responded to me. One man, whose words never made sense to me, used to follow me down the halls. I felt a closeness to several others, although I could never talk easily to them about Jesus Christ.

As awareness of my gift has increased, I've grown in sensitivity to the guidance of the Holy Spirit. I'm learning to say "Yes" when I feel my gifts fit. I'm also learning to say "No."

For example, months ago my friend Charlie called. "Cec, here's a great opportunity for you. For almost a year I've been working at starting a new church. They're ready for a full-time pastor. I'd like to recommend you because I don't intend to stay."

Of course, Charlie's endorsement flattered me. His enthusiasm excited me, as he explained that they had a congregation of nearly one hundred people, already owned ten acres of land, had a significant amount banked for their first building unit. They had also committed themselves to give 50 percent of their income to benevolent causes.

Quite a tempting offer, but I refused.

First, I did not feel it was God's timing for me to leave the church where I am now the pastor. But the second reason loomed even stronger: it wasn't the kind of congregation with whom I felt my particular gifts would be most used. Charlie made one statement which convinced me (even though I earnestly prayed for guidance). He called them an affluent group, and said, "I've always had the ability to get wealthy people excited and involved."

As I continued praying, one thought kept coming to me: I've been able to get the average or even lower-middle-class person excited about the Lord. That's when I knew the other church wasn't where my gifts would work best.

Naturally, making a statement like that always carries danger. One reason is that we never know how God might choose to stretch us or to extend our spiritual gifts. Or he may put us in a situation where we become aware of gifts we didn't know about.

This happened to me when the Lord called us to Kenya. Until I actually sensed that call, it never seriously occurred to me that God wanted me on the mission field. My thinking was influenced, I suppose, by reports I'd heard from the missionaries themselves. Not only did one have to be both a teacher and preacher (that didn't bother me), but also a full-fledged mechanic, or at least a person with some manual dexterity (that left me out!). My view of missionary work was partially distorted, of course. The Spirit never endowed me with the ability to work well with my hands. He did, however, stretch my gifts in other ways. I adjusted to a different culture, learned two languages, and realized a deeper faith in Christ.

Generally, God calls us to work in areas for which he has given us gifts. That knowledge provides great freedom as we seek guidance.

As I become aware of God's working through spiritual enablements, I've tried approaching volunteers in the church on this basis. For example, recently the church school superintendent notified me that we needed teachers in two departments. Instead of calling people who had taught before, or trying to think of those who might be willing to try, I made it a matter of prayer for two days.

"Lord, we have people in our church who can teach. They have your gifts and can do a good job. Show me whom to call."

At the end of two days I called Mary and Morris. Their reply: "We'd love to." The next day I called Trish, who said she'd pray about it. A week later, she called and said, "Yes, I'll teach."

On the other hand, I once asked a woman in our congregation to head up a project, because I knew she was energetic and faithful. She listened as I told her what the job involved, how long it would take, and what its purpose was. Then she said, "Cec, I would be willing to do it because you ask me. But frankly, it's not an area where I feel I have the ability."

Translated into more spiritual terms, she could easily have said, "God has not gifted me." And she rightly refused. The person who eventually handled the project did a great job.

As I talk to people, I now urge them to examine themselves: "Pray, and ask the Lord to show you what gifts he wants you to exercise." Being aware of our special areas of ability doesn't guarantee we're always in God's will. But it does provide one more way to discern what the Spirit wants us to say and to do.

I've found this approach helpful, because it means we no longer have to recruit people simply because of their availability or their willingness. Now we can consider the giftedness of the individual. Once a person says, "I have the gift of administration," then I can say, "Would you pray about being in charge of our spring retreat?"

Individuals also become more aware of their special function within the church. They acknowledge their spiritual limitations, but also appreciate the areas of their giftedness.

For example, I'm no evangelist. I've done the work of an evangelist—and effectively—during my missionary days. When I first went to Africa, evangelistic work ranked as top priority. Along with half a dozen Africans, I helped start at least ten churches. But one day two realizations hit me. First, the nationals evangelized better than I did. They knew the right turn of phrase; they sensed the moment to call for commitment. They also reaped better results. Second, I had teaching ability not being used but badly needed.

From that time on, my top priority centered on setting up training courses for evangelists, pastors, teachers, and lay workers. I taught them the principles and sent them out to do the work. God has endowed me with the gift of teaching. I affirm and use that gift. When I moved into my area of usefulness, both the Africans and I felt a greater sense of fulfillment. We also saw more far-reaching results.

Knowing our spiritual gifts is worthwhile for one reason alone—it helps us know where God wants to use us. Our relationship to Christ grows, not only as he strengthens us, but also as we use our gifts to strengthen others!

22.

Know Your Gifts

"You said a lot about spiritual gifts," Ron told me. *"Really* challenged me. But—" He hesitated, and finally blurted out, "but how—how do you know your spiritual gifts? How can I know what spiritual abilities the Lord has given me?"

Ron asked a good question, one we all need to consider.

I don't have any foolproof answers. I do have suggestions on how to discover our spiritual gifts. As we pray for God's guidance, as we look at these suggestions, we can learn more about knowing our own areas of giftedness.

1. *Know Yourself.* Who said that originally? Everyone from Socrates to Marcus Aurelius to Shakespeare's Polonius gets credit. But no matter, it's still important. As we know ourselves, we begin seeing the areas in which God blesses and empowers us.

We can ask ourselves, "What kind of activities get me enthusiastic?" That's a major clue. What kind of things bore us? That's obviously not our gifted area.

For example, once we needed work done on the church-owned house in which we lived. Pug, a faithful member of the congregation, said, "We'll take care of it for you."

I mumbled something about not being able to help much. Pug smiled and said, "You take care of the spiritual things around the church, and I'll take care of this. You do what you do best, and I'll do what I do best."

That's how I see spiritual gifts operating. We do God's will by using the gifts he bestows. We also avoid the areas in which he has not endowed us.

As I mentally review my past, I remember experiences that excited me. I recall times when I felt adequate to my tasks. In my first career years, God put me in a position to teach, not only in Africa but in American classrooms. I taught elementary grades, high school, and even college. I can't recall a time while teaching when I didn't feel I belonged—even on those days when it seemed as though the lesson didn't meet with high response.

Not only education, but all my areas of satisfaction have been people-centered. Every job I've enjoyed involved having people around me. On the other hand, during my early military days, I had a job I detested. The officer in charge put me at a desk in the far corner of a large room. The closest person worked at least thirty feet away. I typed reports all day. No one came to my desk. I had almost no contact with the others in the office. Even telephone calls involved only business matters. After two months, I asked for a transfer, and the officer agreed. I soon learned all of the fourteen different jobs in the department, so that I could fill in as people went on leave, transferred, or became sick. Being in the middle of all that people-type activity made me enjoy my work. I needed to be around other human beings.

2. *Pray.* That seems obvious, but I wonder how often we actually ask God to show us our gifts. If God endows us, he expects us to use our spiritual abilities.

A verse I learned during the first months after my conversion has helped me in this area: "If any of you lacks wisdom, let him ask God, who gives to all men generously and without reproaching, and it will be given him" (James 1:5).

I suggest also a daily prayer for understanding. I have a friend who, after getting excited about spiritual gifts, prayed one prayer every day for several months. It went like this:

> Lord, I am yours. You have given me gifts.
> Help me recognize them. Help me exercise them.

Simple but direct. He's now living in a deeper dimension of

closeness with the Lord. "I don't have all the answers to God's will," he told me, "but at least I know more about what God wants me to do. It's easier to hear God speak, because I'm constantly making myself available to his leading."

3. *Get others' responses.* Carl tried just about every job in the church. He made a disastrous attempt to teach, and gave it up after four Sundays. He tried the choir, and finally the choir director kindly said, "Carl, sing as softly as you can. That way I hope you'll *listen* to the bass section. You're singing so loudly you throw them off." Carl didn't last long in the choir. He volunteered to organize several committees, and they floundered. At one time, he thought heading into the ministry was the Lord's leading. But poor Carl couldn't even stand up in church and give an announcement without garbling it.

Everyone had gotten used to misfitted Carl (not that anyone called him that). But one thing about Carl I appreciated was his willingness to help with small but urgent situations. When we needed someone to take an elderly person to the doctor, Carl loved doing it. We regularly collect used clothing for a community agency. Carl would gladly fill his car and make two trips with the clothing. Carl heard that we needed a new typewriter in the office. He checked all the local dealers, presented me with a list that showed what was available, the prices, and whether the machines were new or rebuilt.

One evening after our sharing group Carl seemed a bit low, and Esther came up to him. "You know, Carl, I was thinking about you the other day. Have you ever considered that God has given you the ministry of helper?"

He didn't seem to understand.

Esther flipped out her Bible and read 1 Corinthians 12:28: "And God has appointed in the church first apostles, second prophets, third teachers, then workers of miracles, then healers, helpers, administrators, speakers in various kinds of tongues."

Esther went on to say, "That's how I see you, Carl—a helper. You're the kind of person we can call on to give a hand when we need transportation, or—"

"Yeah, I think I know what you mean."

That encounter meant much to Carl's spiritual growth. He had been trying every possible kind of involvement in church leadership Because of his willingness, people let him try—once. They never wanted him doing anything a second time. Now Carl has found a niche. He filled the gap, doing the little errands and jobs that some of the others didn't want.

In the Presbyterian Church of which I am a minister, we have certain steps people go through before they enter into the professional ministry. The first step is to declare to the elders of the church their intention. The elders, representing the congregation, must concur in the person's call. The governing body of the local church has the responsibility to assess a person's suitability (that is, giftedness) before he or she prepares for the ministry.

I'd like to see more of this in any form of ministry in our churches.

Think of the more efficient way we could work if each person declared, "These are my spiritual gifts, as best I understand them." That would keep the door open for expanded ministry, but also limit involvement where God may not wish to lead them. We're often *pushed* into positions, rather than *led* there by the Spirit!

4. Evaluate. As we involve ourselves in discovering God's will, we need to examine what's happening.

Years ago I met a man who mentioned he had been the head usher in his church for more than twenty years. "It's what I like doing better than anything else," he said. "When people come in, I get the privilege of greeting them, of introducing myself, and welcoming them. I'm there if any emergencies arise."

As I listened, I noticed how his eyes sparkled.

That's part of the test of evaluation. How does the person feel he or she is doing? How do others respond? What kind of results do we see?

5. Be open. Jesus said, "He who is faithful in a very little is faithful also in much" (Luke 16:10). The parable of the talents teaches us that when we use what we have, God increases our resources. That's a principle of the spiritual life.

I've seen it in myself. Take the area of my writing. I've always enjoyed writing, but never thought seriously about having anything published. After going to Africa, we sent letters to our friends, telling them of the work. One Midwestern magazine with a circulation of less than ten thousand contacted me: "How about sending us a letter each month? We'd like to print it in our magazine." For over five years, they published letters and pictures telling about our work. Each month I worked over the letter, sometimes changing and retyping it as many as six times. But I still never thought about writing professionally.

In 1971, I enrolled in a course, "Writing for the Masses"— not because of any literary ambitions, but because Charlie Shedd taught it. He's an author I had read and liked; I would have taken any course he taught. At the end of the quarter, he called six of us aside. "I think you folks have talent. Why don't you do something about it? Maybe start a writer's group."

I prayed about Charlie's suggestion, and that night we formed what came to be known as the Scribe Tribe—which continued nine years. During the early months of forming and participating with the group, I knew that God had called me to write. I made a promise to him: "Lord, I'll work to become the best writer I'm capable of being." I'm still trying to improve.

6. *Exercise it*. I have no doubts—the Lord gave me the gift to write (even though that is not specifically mentioned in the Bible as one of the gifts). But I don't sit at the typewriter, pray, and then listen as the words flow directly from heaven. I pray—some days more than others—about my writing. I plead for God's guidance and ask him to make my finished product honor him.

But I also do the work. I pound the keys. I rewrite and edit. That also entails doing research. Sometimes it means tearing up a whole day's work and starting over. I critically look at each page, then I set it aside for a few days. When I read the chapter again, I always see ways to improve it.

Not once have I ever read over anything I have written without making changes. I keep trying to improve my style and the content. Because of the desire to improve, I'm a better scribe for the Lord today than I was a year ago.

That's true with many writers. It may be that's why, when you ask, "What's your best book?" they answer, "The next one.' God gives us the gift to communicate on paper; now we have to improve it *by exercising it,* by praying about how to do the next book or article better, by thinking about it often.

This applies to all areas of God's gifts. After I teach a Sunday school class, replay action goes on in my head. How could I have taught it better? How can it be improved next week? I don't slip into depression when the class doesn't measure up to what I wanted it to be. I merely say, "Okay, Cec, next time you'll do a better job."

Occasionally a person says, "I believe in spiritual gifts. God just overlooked me when he passed them around."

I don't believe that! Some exercise more gifts than others, but no one is passed over!

Not even people like Josh, who once said those very words to me.

Josh used to walk around as though apologizing for being alive. He was one of the most self-effacing people I'd ever known. He attended various activities at the church, but took no leadership in any of them. He wasn't good at sports, and felt too shy to usher, teach, or head up a committee. But on two different occasions I saw him get cars started in the parking lot. Once he got the hood open, Josh took command. He knew exactly what to do.

Later I mentioned a plumbing problem at our house. "I'll come over and look at it," he said casually. He came the next day, surveyed the situation, took out a few tools, and within minutes had solved the problem.

"Josh," I said, after thanking him profusely, "you really are gifted. You have that marvelous ability to work with your hands."

He smiled self-consciously and finally said, "Yeah, that's right. Give me anything to do with my hands and I'll do it—and do a good job. Just don't ask me to talk to people."

For several minutes we discussed spiritual gifts. I explained to Josh that, as I saw him, he had a great gift from God. He admitted he had never thought of it that way before.

Although our conversation continued several minutes longer, I don't remember anything more except his final words: "I guess God didn't forget me after all, did he?"

23.

Of Course God Led Me . . .
Didn't He?

I was visiting another church with friends, and a portion of the service centered on giving testimonies. Various people stood up and told of how God had guided them on recent days.

Afterwards my friend said, "How can they be so positive? Sometimes I'm absolutely sure it's God. But most of the time, I just don't know. I pray, and I really want to follow God, but . . ." And in his pause I understood. Sometimes we're just not sure.

Maybe guidance is never meant to be a totally sure thing. Perhaps the element of faith needs always to be mixed in. That means we can never verify all our decisions. We go on and do the best we can. Sometimes we'll never know if we made the right choice. Our commitment to Jesus Christ can only assure us that, if we're attempting to follow his guidance, he won't let us go too far astray.

Joseph in the Old Testament obviously didn't understand God's plan until later in his life. While he was still a young man, his brothers sold him into slavery. He languished in prison because of the lies of a seductive woman. Later, after becoming second in command of Egypt, he saved his entire family during the years of famine in Israel. After their father's death, Joseph summed it up for his brothers: "You meant evil against me; but

God meant it for good, to bring it about that many people should be kept alive, as they are today" (Gen. 50:20).

That's how God often works—through the unexpected. And we often don't recognize the happening as guidance from the Holy Spirit. It's only after the fact—sometimes many years later—that we think about the incident and say, "God led me, didn't he?"

Haven't we all heard stories of chance encounters, brief conversations—how reading a book or missing an airplane have changed the directions of a life? Yet, at the time, the person whose life was changed didn't see the incident as God's handiwork.

In his autobiography, Dr. Albert Schweitzer tells how he was trying to decide what to do with his life. One night, while still in college, he picked up a green-covered magazine from the Paris Missionary Society. He intended to lay it aside so that he could get on with his studies, but he absent-mindedly opened it to an article by the president, Alfred Boegner. In the article the author appealed for workers, saying they couldn't continue their work in Gabon, a northern province of the Congo. Schweitzer later said, "My search was over." He had no way of knowing then that the entire course of his own life, and that of the world, would be changed by the chance reading of a magazine article.

Often it is only in retrospect that we can see how the Lord has guided our lives.

Looking back over my life, I can think of several experiences, in which I was led by the Holy Spirit, but in which I was unaware of his direction at the moment they occurred. I moved ahead because it seemed the sensible thing to do. Only later, by reflection, could I see how skillfully the Lord had guided.

Near the end of my second year in seminary, I received a phone call on a late Saturday afternoon from the dean of students. He needed a student to preach at a local church the next day. They had gone through the list of seniors, and were now going down the list of juniors—and I was next on the list. Was there any way I could go on such a short notice?

"Yes, certainly," I answered, and began preparing.

I went the next day, preached, and before I left the church the four church officers, after huddling in a corner of the room, came to me. "Mr. Murphey, we'll soon need a new part-time minister here. Would you accept this?"

I said yes without even praying about it. First, I needed the income. Second, I had been in seminary nearly two years with no outlet for preaching or teaching on an ongoing basis.

That experience changed the whole direction of my life. I had planned to complete seminary, continue on for a doctoral degree, and eventually teach in a college or seminary. Why not? I had previously taught. My work had been largely in the field of education. It seemed natural.

However, during the months I remained at Clifton Church, a change took place in me. I loved being a pastor. That was strange, because I had never considered that as a serious option before. I never did get my doctoral degree—and I've never regretted it.

In retrospect, I realize God altered the course of my life with that decision.

We all have times when we've prayed, when we've used every available means to know the right directions, but still lack certainty. In those cases, we have to wait until we can look backwards and then discern the hand of God guiding our decisions.

Those of us who know Christ can look back and see the methods God used to bring us to himself. Some of us came out of a sense of need, others by having someone share and thereby having our appetite whetted.

When we were missionaries in Africa, people often told us, "I was walking along the road, and I heard your happy singing. I stood outside and listened. Then, when the preacher spoke, I thought he could see me outside, and he spoke directly to me."

More recently, a woman shared this with me. Friends had been urging her to attend worship with them. They belonged to a religious, but not particularly Christian group. She agreed to attend, and they gave her directions. She drove to our church and, thinking she had come to where her friends attended, went inside. She never saw her friends, but that didn't seem to upset her. She attended the early service, and then someone said, "Come and join us in Sunday school." She did. Minutes before the class concluded, the teacher said something about "us Presbyterians," and the woman burst out laughing, "Is this the *Presbyterian* church?" She then explained what had happened. However, she liked the people and the friendly spirit. She came back the following Sunday, and then the next. One day, months later, she said, "You know, I really believe in Jesus Christ." She went on to explain all that had happened in the past and said, "Just think, if I had not gone to the wrong church. . . ." She stopped and smiled, "No, I think God led me to the right church, but I just didn't know it then."

We have to admit that some guidance can be seen only with hindsight. It reminds me of that old song my mother sang, "Farther Along," which ends, "We'll understand it all by and by."

I'm not offering the old standby phrase, "God will explain it all someday," and I'm not attempting to say that God makes everything clear to us—now or ever. Part of the mystery of being a follower of Christ is that not everything makes sense. Many happenings have no explanation. God doesn't *have* to tell us the *whys* of our situations; we have no inherent right to explanations.

Experiences happen to all of us which never quite make sense. But for some of those unusual ones, we appreciate and understand them only in retrospect. And the fact that we can look back and see his hand gives us cause for rejoicing.

Only this morning a woman sat in my office and talked for almost an hour. If anyone had tasted the dregs of hell, she had. Twice in a period of five years she had been hospitalized for an emotional breakdown. Her suicide attempts, by medication overdosing or by slitting her wrists, totaled eight. But somehow she had come through all of that. Today, years later, she's a radiant witness for Jesus Christ.

As she sat in my office, she said, "Sometimes I feel ashamed and guilty—not wanting people to know what I went through. But most of the time, I'm glad about it. I understand myself better. I can also help other people."

I thought of four different women this transformed Christian had helped through severe mental anguish. She had helped because she understood and had gone through it herself.

While she didn't actually say the words, I think she could easily have said, "Now that I'm well, I can see where the Lord had his hand on me all along. I know God guided me and brought me out."

She can say it now. But I recall that when I first met her she screamed at me, "If there's a God in this crazy world, where is he? Why did he let me go crazy? Why doesn't he stop it all?"

I still can't answer all her questions. And I don't suppose she can, either. Yet both of us know this much: as we look backward, we know that the Lord walked by her side every step of the way.